They Called Me *Otherwise*

Stories of growing up in Africa, Scotland and Canada

Bill Galloway, alias Wullie

Copyright © 2005 Bill Galloway

All rights reserved. No written or illustrated part of this book may be reproduced, except for brief quotations in articles or reviews, without permission from the publisher.

Library and Archives Canada Cataloguing in Publication

Galloway, Bill, 1947-
They called me otherwise : stories of growing up in Africa, Scotland and Canada / Bill Galloway.
ISBN 1-894694-37-6

1. Galloway, Bill, 1947-. 2. Scottish Canadians--Biography.
3. National characteristics, Scottish. 4. Businessmen--British Columbia--Vancouver--Biography. I. Title.

FC3847.26.G34A3 2005   971.1'3304'092   C2005-903137-9

Editor: Graham Hayman
Proofreader: Neall Calvert
Book and cover design: Gordon Finlay

First printing June 2005

Granville Island
Publishing
212-1656 Duranleau
Vancouver, BC, Canada V6H 3S4
Tel: (604) 688-0320 Toll free: 1-877-688-0320
www.GranvilleIslandPublishing.com

TABLE OF CONTENTS

Introduction: Ma Name's *Wullie*   1

1. Criminal Connections   13
    My Family from 4 Billion Years BC to 1947
    Large Ears
    Criminal Connections
    Hooch Mon

2. Easy Living: Johannesburg 1947 to 1958   24
    Manners? Bananas?
    Plenty of Peaches and Plums
    Gold on Them Thar Tables
    Joking with Uncle Jimmy
    Christmas Dinner for a Stranger
    Just Missing the Royal Connection
    Oor Wullie and The Telly

3. My Early Education about Birds and Bees: Scotland 1958 to 1960   35
    Giving up Oor Wullie and South Africa
    Strathallan: One Question Too Many
    Forever Naïve
    Waxworks Handshake
    School Food: A Doggy Delicacy
    Strawberries and Cream
    Lost In The Fog

4. **The Hopeless Athlete: South Africa 1961 to 1964** 45
    Another Big Upheaval
    Commander Wullie
    Tortoise Rescues
    Boys, Insects and Spiders
    Is The Moon Mendacious?
    Learning to Appreciate Gourmet Cuisine
    Rugby Teams: Who Wants Wullie?
    Finding the Athlete Within
    The Master of Physical Education
    I Get My Stripes
    Are You Blind?
    African Royal Wedding

5. **Wullie Loses His Brains: Free at Last 1965 to 1969** 67
    "University is Not the Place for Him"
    Campus Years: Facing Apartheid
    Uncle Jimmy's Gourmet South Africa
    A Second Chance for the Bar of Gold
    Save Every Golf Tee
    Arrested for Carol Singing?
    Physics was Not My Subject
    Final Reckoning with University
    The Real World?
    Black Humour

6. **Scotland Regained: Saint Andrews 1969 to 1973** 81
    Leaving South Africa Yet Again
    A Lesson in Chutzpah
    Probably Just A Coincidence
    You Met Where?
    Mr. Birrell's Grocery: "Ye'll Have Anotherr Glass?"
    Eros at Madame Tussauds
    Politically Correct Language

    First Home: Westburn Wynd
    Sunday Post to the Rescue
    Cowardice, Courage and the Comic John Cleese
    "Is This Yoor Spo'lump?"
    First Christmas Married
    Wine Connections: Starting a Tradition

7. Return to the Land My Great-grandfather Farmed   103
    Graduate School in Canada
    A Home for One's Children
    Sex Ed. in Jail
    Putting My Best into a Ph.D.

8. In Business in Vancouver   111
    Play-acting for a Living
    Bu$ine$$ Lunch
    Success and More Success
    Family Threads are Rewoven
    Film Stars Invade My Gym
    The Sheecret of Shuksessh
    "Call Hotel Security!"
    "Just Who Are You Guys, Anyway?"
    Three Strikes: Dining Out in Prince George

9. Family Foibles in Vancouver   134
    Melanie's Cakes with a Difference
    Fermions les Bosons
    The Weeks That Were
    Mr. Galloway's Garden and Mrs. Rabbit
    The Floating Keys
    Bilinguility
    Night-times and Other Times in Hospitals
    Where Were You That Day?
    On Friendship

AUTHOR'S NOTE

These are my stories, and I have told them often. Family members have rolled their eyeballs when I repeated some of them. Here they are again in print, somewhat polished, so that succeeding generations may repeat these Galloway stories in their turn.

The stories show how full my life has been. So, from a husband, a father, a grandpère, a highly skilled bumbler, a business colleague and a friend, I say to all who have helped make it so full: Thank you—and keep on filling it, please.

Many who have made huge contributions to my life are not mentioned here at length. No slight is intended. This book grew out of a bunch of disconnected stories into a more ordered narrative, but it is not a full autobiography. There are still other tales to tell, at other times.

Permission for the picture of Oor Wullie sitting on his bucket is kindly given by *The Sunday Post*, © The Sunday Post, D. C. Thomson & Co. Ltd.

The excellent drawings of the chimpanzee, the runners, the boys in the dormitory, the back of the wine store, the moon and the restaurant all capture the mood of these incidents so well. They were done by Ljuba Levstek. These drawings are Copyright © Ljuba Levstek.

The information on my grandfather leaving home at an early age and travelling to South Africa, among other places, is contained in the September 1943 edition of *The South African Builder*. Thank you, South African Builder.

I want to acknowledge the following for the hard work they have put into the book:
- Graham Hayman for extracting more stories than I had realised existed in me and sharpening their focus;
- Neall Calvert for his fine attention to the details of grammar, style and content;
- Gordon Finlay for his keen ability to synthesise pictures and text into a book;
- Jo Blackmore of Granville Island Publishing for encouraging me to grow a book out of a collection of family folklore.

Three other people helped me immensely and also deserve to be acknowledged:
- Melanie Galloway for tirelessly reading and rereading my stories;
- Stewart Hoar for taking the photograph of Wullie in his kilt on the bucket;
- Doctor Jennifer Hoar for doing early editing, making corrections and providing support.

Vancouver, 2005

©The Sunday Post, D.C. Thomson & Co. Ltd.

Oor Wullie, from the Scottish *Sunday Post*

INTRODUCTION
Ma Name's Wullie

When very young, I heard my mother saying that I was called "William Robert Otherwise Bill." Not knowing that Otherwise was merely a word, I assumed it was also one of my names. My nature has always been to exist apart from the herd, and in that respect I am certainly "otherwise." So this set of stories is written by "Wullie"—of this world, yet not quite of this universe, often living in a naïve Brigadoon, but also knowing I have a place, and laughing both at the world around and at myself within it.

My father often called me Wullie, though "Billious" was another nickname he projected upon me. As you can imagine, I prefer the less sickly Wullie.

Why Wullie and not Willie? The spelling reflects Scottish pronunciation. "Oor Wullie" (or as the English would say it, "Our Willie") is also a cartoon character from the Scottish *Sunday Post* newspaper. As a boy of about six, while living in South Africa, I picked up the cartoon book collection of Oor Wullie. I felt very at ease with him, and so set about learning the strange words and accent that comprise the Glasgow dialect.

Oor Wullie has been a Scottish icon since 1939. He is the creation of a talented cartoonist, Dudley Dexter Watkins. Wullie's an inner-city (probably Glasgow) boy; he speaks a vernacular which, albeit English, can sound far from it. Although I was named William, after my granddad, I also think of my shadow character as Wullie, whom Glaswegians will recognise. While I was living in South Africa, this wee character helped introduce me to my Glaswegian heritage and dialect.

The Glasgow accent is produced by swallowing all words into the back of the throat and speaking without moving the lips. Glaswegians would make excellent ventriloquists, though I think that this failure to move the mouth is at least as much due to a fear of false teeth falling flat on the floor, as it is to the accent. Try to utter the name "Willie" without moving your lips and gulp the vowel sound to the back of your throat. This will help you achieve the correct pronunciation of "Wullie." It isn't "Wollie," nor "Willie," nor "Woollie." I can speak it today, ingesting those words into the back of my throat, dropping all the consonants and intoning the sing-song lowering of the voice on the penultimate word or syllable.

The family of Oor Wullie the cartoon character are not well off, but they are never destitute. His escapades are weak, especially compared to the spider men of today. Even when the other comic stories featured radio-controlled toys for boys, Oor Wullie had not much more than an upturned bucket upon which to sit. He's a happy boy despite this and epitomises the Scots, who get on with life and make do with so little. Even his pet is a "wee moose" (mouse), not a horse or even a dog. He does all the usual boyish deeds: fighting with his friends, making up, escaping from school, enjoying sweeties (candy, to North Americans) and shunning the company of girls. Oor Wullie has been a pre-teenage boy for over fifty years. He lives as part of the world and also apart from it, in something of a time warp. His great appeal is that ordinary folk can see their simple lives in Oor Wullie.

Occasionally he steps outside his stories. In one of them, he and his pals want the autograph of the cowboy hero "Tex

Introduction

Rogers." The friends are booted from the hotel room, but Wullie sneaks back in dressed as a plumber. Tex finds him and immediately asks Wullie for his autograph. Like all the stories, it is not side-splittingly funny retold in prose. Wullie gives his autograph and brags to his jealous chums outside that Tex had recognised him from the *Sunday Post* newspaper. The hero Tex seeks out the antihero. Wullie steps outside and addresses himself as a character in the newspaper.

That's how I see my nature too, almost as a bystander watching myself interact with the world. So some of these stories are written in the third person, with Wullie as that character. It's my way of looking at myself in different situations. It's still me, but observed by myself from outside my own skin.

Oor Wullie was uniquely Wullie, but was also very Scottish, as I am myself. Wullie helped me to learn about my origins, roots, genetics, historical context and thereby to understand myself. Although I was born in South Africa, I never doubted that I was Scottish. We always referred to Glasgow and the family there as "home." As Scots abroad, we never felt as though we were "undesirables"; the Scots are for the most part welcomed and welcoming. Several traits assist them in being so accepted. What are those qualities?

The Scots are explorers, and not only through this cartoon character but also through the Scots personality and history have I come to explore myself and so understand my journey. Many Scots families left their homeland because economic considerations forced them away. The Highland Clearances, after the defeat of Bonnie Prince Charlie at Culloden in 1746, saw many thousands emigrate to Australia, America, Canada and South Africa over the next hundred years and more. Life is a metaphorical expedition and also a literal one.

Some Scots left home to spread Christianity to the savage world. If we find that hard to stomach today, substitute democracy or perhaps women's rights. If we believe it worthwhile to promote those ideals, we might have an inkling of how Mungo Park, who went to Africa as a missionary, felt. At his first sermon in Scotland, on reaching the pulpit, this timid, brave Scot stammered, "Friends, I've forgotten all I was going to say." He went on to explore Africa, surviving expeditions when few other white men did.

We Galloways have also been travellers, as my tales will explore, and I suspect other Scots left home because they couldn't stand the endless diet of lumpy oatmeal porridge. In my formative years, when I was removed from South Africa to endure the rigours of Scottish boarding school, I had to take a personal and brave stance against porridge. Our family members seem to have oscillated around Scotland, Canada and Africa since the 1870s.

Often thrust out from their homeland, with little economic wealth, the Scots used their humour to assist them in their new worlds, both to entertain and to gain acceptance. It's hard to remain angry with an enemy when you have just shared a joke. The Scots' self-deprecating style is sometimes successful because it does not challenge the other party too directly. Although the Scots can be passionate and earnest, they usually don't take themselves too seriously.

In Canada there has been the occasional ruckus in schools over men from India wearing ceremonial daggers. And in workplaces, knives of any kind seem inappropriate to Western culture. Recently in France, there was a fuss over young Islamic women students being forbidden to wear headscarfs while attending public school. Can you imagine the Scots making a national crisis about boys being forbidden to wear *sgian dhus* to school? The sgian dhu is a wee black sheathed dagger usually carried close to the right knee, slid into the stocking top. We would not see grand priestie people proclaiming fatwas against such a prohibition. It just doesn't seem very Scottish.

The Scots have a well-worn reputation for being frugal. This

Introduction

jibe invariably paints them as having tightly drawn purses. I'm a thrifty person myself, disliking waste. Of course this trait comes from my roots, and Scots make themselves more accepted by first acknowledging the joke against them. As in all caricatures, there is an ounce of truth and a dose of exaggeration. Scottish folk had to be thrifty, for they had so little. Even Scottish land—at least the English so decided— was more suited to sheep than to other agriculture.

The Scots can be generous and hospitable, sometimes in the smallest of ways, and also in the grandest. Andrew Carnegie, railway baron though he was, gave away huge fortunes not only to his native Scotland but internationally too. Carnegie Mellon, a research university for the children of working-class Pittsburghers, and eastside Vancouver's Carnegie Library building are typical examples, among many.

The choices of a university and a library are not accidental. Scots generally lay great store by education. My grandfather valued learning too as a portal to economic success, but also because it was right. Starting as a bricklayer, he became a stonemason and eventually graduated as an architect.

The Scots didn't have much raw material, so they had to become their own resource, and they accomplished this in part by higher education. In this they were immeasurably assisted by John Knox, a firebrand Scots Protestant fundamentalist. Intolerant, bigoted, dogmatic—he was all of these. He wanted each man to seek his own salvation with God, without intercession by costly priests. For that purpose, it became essential that all wee girls and boys be taught to read for themselves. How else could they know the truth direct from the Bible, for interpreters were not to be trusted. John Knox may have thereby precipitated the ultimate sin, alienation from God, assisting people to enter into their own state of knowledge. But this most liberal tradition is one with which the Scots proudly daub themselves.

So although the Galloway roots were in farmyards and

then stonemasonry, all the family were encouraged to take every opportunity for gaining an education. My own father, although a businessman and chartered accountant, was also a classics and humanities scholar. He studied Greek, Latin and political economy at Glasgow University and valued these as much as his profession. In fact, they were part of his professionalism.

Human history shows that creativity arises from putting diverse ideas together. Liam Hudson, an Edinburgh psychologist, has written cogently on the whole area of creativity, an additional arm of intelligence often not detected on the linear radar screens of scholastic achievement tests. The Scots' approach to education—that all people should be literate to enable them to think for themselves; and an emphasis on broad studies—tells us why the Scots did so well in so many endeavours, like engineering (Thomas Telford), exploration (David Livingstone) and medicine (Joseph Lister).

When Scottish pupils come to the final school years, they sit "highers," not the English "A levels." Highers are much more of a broad brush; Scots might take six highers where the English student would take two or three A levels. There is more emphasis on general education. I've followed this tradition by getting degrees in both arts and science.

The practical outcomes of Scots education are some notable achievements. Think of the inventors James Watt, steam engine; Alexander Graham Bell, telephone; James Logie Baird, television; Alexander Fleming, penicillin. These were giants upon whom we have built our technologically successful existence today. The Clyde River, flowing through Glasgow west towards the sea, was once synonymous with shipbuilding. At one time Glasgow and surrounding towns held the greatest concentration of shipbuilding expertise in the world and with it, engineering. The Scots have had a big impact for such a small country.

This is an intimidating legacy and Wullie Galloway felt that

Introduction

he had to live up to it. At times it was daunting, but Wullie did go on to study higher mathematics and statistics, philosophy and psychology and become a professional accountant. He then practised in none of these, though also in all of them, by working into a career within computer science.

Scottish education has produced its share of world-class philosophers, for example David Hume and his friend Adam Smith. Many of us associate Adam Smith with the book that allegedly supports capitalism, *The Wealth of Nations*. However, that acknowledges only half of Smith. His other great work was *The Theory of Moral Sentiment*. Here the themes of benevolence and sympathy with one's fellow man are dominant. Smith is often wrongly stereotyped.

As a young adult, I studied philosophy at the University of Saint Andrews, including Hume, Smith, Locke and Ayer. Hume is regarded as one of the great empiricists, who believe that experience is supremely important. So scientists in that tradition want to see externally verified proof for theories, rather than trying to deduce principles from other knowledge. The Cartesian philosophy of Descartes, in contrast to the empirical outlook, is famous for the saying, "I think, therefore I am."

Personally, I think of human qualities as embodying the ability to understand humour: "I laugh, therefore I am." If Scots have been the butt of many jokes, they have also developed a self-belittling way of defusing the punch line by acknowledging the tease against themselves. Scottish humour is pawky and often subtle. The word "pawk" is Scottish for trick, so pawky means "with a dry sense of humour." Sometimes one is not even sure if a joke is in play: if you recognise it, it is, and if you don't, it never was. As with their money, Scots are thrifty with their humour. You should not need great dollops, just wee soupçons.

As people who often had to make their fun by entertaining themselves, the Scots would sometimes play party games, including charades; it was not uncommon to find ordinary families enjoying the mockery and indulgence which comes from acting and impersonating. Sir Sean Connery is among the world's best-known actors today. And many of us have enjoyed the humour and pathos too of Robert Carlyle in *The Full Monty*. But the Scots are not always humorous with tongue in cheek. Ewan McGregor in *Trainspotting* exposes a dark side.

    Acting is of course not uniquely Scottish, but we use it to rise out of poverty or from under English subjugation. We also employ it just to have fun, and sometimes to make a dig against the establishment. My grandfather would entertain family and friends in his home by reciting from memory long excerpts from Shakespeare. We're not a family of performers, but the tradition of being a good storyteller and raconteur runs strongly. As hosts, we were taught to be entertaining. Some of the following stories show this tradition, where at times we aren't really sure when we are playing ourselves, or performing roles.

    A website containing Scots comedian Billy Connolly's "Life Lessons" includes in the list: "Salute nobody." This reminds us to be wary of those who try and impose authority over us. My distrust of these is just the same, although my style is totally different. Sometimes, by pretending to be someone who you are not, you can become that character, at least for a while, thereby enriching your own life. So it was with Wullie.

    Another common Scots trait is tenacity. Alexander Selkirk, the real-life model for Robinson Crusoe, was a Scot who survived for over four years on Juan Fernandez Island off the Chilean coast. Following the Highland Clearances, many Scots were forced to live on meagre rations, some of them becoming "kelpers" who harvested seaweed. They took almost nothing and they adapted to survive on it. Much more recently, Scottish Peter MacSporran for a time maintained an excellent farm in Zimbabwe. Run off it by Robert Mugabe's

Introduction

affiliates, he moved on to Zambia and has been a key resource in revitalising farming in that country.

One cannot talk of the Scots without mentioning their bloody-mindedness, though a more polite word would be "persistence." They even have their own adjective for it: "thrawn," as in "he was a thrawn adversary." By contrast, Scotland is often thought to be more socialist than the rest of Britain, because they learned to survive by helping each other out. The unions wanted workers' rights to combat managerial greed, and their stubborn natures appeared often in the political foment along the banks of the River Clyde, so that it became known as "Red Clydeside."

Along with their more benevolent virtues, the Scots sometimes exported their politically combative styles, for example, in the Canadian Postal Workers Union head, Joe Davidson. If today the union movement parodies the very corporate excess it originally sought to dethrone, that does not negate the strides it has achieved in safe working conditions, less-punishing working hours and benefits such as education for workers. Joe's legacies are not only his pugnacious style, but also an education fund.

There is a well-known book entitled *How the Scots Invented the Modern World*, by Arthur Herman. The title is cheeky yet acceptable. Imagine if there were a book entitled *How the Americans Invented the Modern World*. It would be scorned with pejorative adjectives like self-serving, dishonest, bragging and many others. The Scots get away with it partly because the notion of one small group being so influential is somewhat ridiculous. Like with the reputation for thrift, however, there are germs of truth in this title. The Scots have made their influence felt around the world (and not just through whisky). On balance, I can say I'm proud to be counted among them.

Like all good chefs, Scots allow themselves to change the recipe, experiment with it and produce unique concoctions.

They Called Me Otherwise

There is a worthy Scots culinary tradition. It's not all haggis (ground heart, kidneys, liver and lungs with spices and oatmeal inside a sheep's stomach). Consider as well Aberdeen Angus beef, Ayrshire bacon, Scottish lamb, pheasants from the moors and the most delicately flavoured river salmon. Dundee marmalade is the finest to be had. One myth states that this citrus-fruit jam was concocted by Marie Queen of Scots' chef when she was ill, hence the name "Marie Malade." However, the original sweet compote was actually made from Portuguese marmelada, originally a quince jelly.

So who am I and how well do I fit the Scottish persona? My friends might say that I am a successful bumbler, something like Inspector Clouseau at his worst. They might add that I am not to be underestimated, nor as fragile nor as much of an oaf as might initially be thought. While this is not a very flattering self-description, it contains a kernel of who I am. By now you know this won't be a story of a great statesman, surgeon, military genius or athlete. But I'll surprise you and humour you if you share my travels, and along the way I'll show you my pride in a wonderfully rich life.

I was at times a useless scholar and a more hopeless athlete, but those epithets are, with hindsight, unfair. The familiar Scottish pillars of education, stubbornness, thrift, even some innovation, humour, emigration, enjoyment of meat and drink have supported me and those around me. I have known despair and hope, and I rest on a strong philosophical empiricism.

A defining pivot of my life was being sent away from South Africa to boarding school in Scotland. It was an alienation from the comfort of my family, but I survived and grew from it. I experienced the despair of failure, particularly my academic collapse. But while in graduate school, I bought my own tiny house on a shoestring budget and rented out part of it to help pay the mortgage: a most thrifty investment. I could call myself a man of property, William R. Galloway, Esquire.

Introduction

I survived rejection by a major computer company, but my stubborn nature helped me overcome this, so that I can now justly (but quietly) claim a successful career in computing systems.

As a student of mathematical statistics, I don't believe that luck runs out, or that coincidences happen, or that someone is due a string of better times. Life happens. So I poke fun at myself often, when coincidental or serendipitous events challenge my stance. I watch my Wullie alter ego enjoy putting on an act, or mimicking an accent, like Peter Sellers does in the Clouseau films. I have fun seeing Wullie play the fool in public and have occasionally performed roles quite out of character, but even more amusing because Wullie gently chides me. There are episodes where Wullie plays the diplomat at the United Nations, takes the mickey out of a physicist and assumes the mantle of a very senior business executive, just because he could.

The South African political regime influenced me strongly while I was studying at the University of the Witwatersrand. It forced me to take a side, and today I value that immensely. Many who have lived in liberal democracies all their lives know not what they have. I inwardly raged as an adolescent at the injustices in that society, but South Africa caused me to confront the inability to change the status quo, and it helped me to learn that we can always find good people in unexpected places. Being an essentially peaceful man, I learned to use humour in making my way. As an example, some friends and I chose to sing Christmas carols to political prisoners, rather than do anything violent. We acknowledged that not only the prisoners but the jailers too were still human beings....

To sum up the Scot: S is for socialistic, schooled and sincere; C is for canny and careful; O is for otherwise; T is for tenacious and thrawn. Add a dash of humour and stir: that's me.

William Galloway, Wullie's Grandfather

CHAPTER ONE

Criminal Connections

My Family from 4 Billion Years BC to 1947

These stories are approximately autobiographical, but their author inherited family stories too, and I will start with my namesake, Great-great-grandfather William Galloway. He was a farm labourer near Wigtown in the Scottish Lowlands region of Galloway. That's 100 miles from Glasgow, which city I still regard as our family seat. So our family is originally "Galloway de Galloway"—but such grandeur of title is completely at odds with our social status and, more importantly, our self-image.

My Great-grandfather David was filled with our family's adventurous spirit when he sailed for Canada in 1873 on a rickety sailing ship, the *SS St. Patrick*, lately converted to steam. He was accompanied by one six-months-pregnant wife, two weans (wee ones—small children) and his mother. Like many Scots, he left hoping for economic gain.

Grandfather William was born in Nepean, Canada in 1875. Within a decade, beaten partly by the harsh Canadian climate, the family returned to their beloved Scotland. They arrived enhanced, however, for the family trade had risen from farm labourer through ploughman to stonemason. William did not linger in Scotland. He left his home in the district of Dennistoun, Glasgow, at the age of twelve to sail before the mast to Valparaiso and back in 1887. After that, he was off to South Africa for five years, where he worked gaining experience as a builder around 1893.

These stories from my grandfather's time are the canvas for my life and who I am, background tones of whether my family were criminals, of our Scottish sense of humour, pioneering spirit, education and doggedness. Despite forays to Canada and South Africa, we always regarded Glasgow as the family home.

Large Ears

My Grampa William was an ambitious but eccentric man. With a family of four children to support, he left Scotland to work abroad in Ghana, in West Africa, which meant that he was absent from his Glasgow home for long periods. He helped forge Thomson Moir and Galloway, a construction company in West Africa. Although Glasgow based, he lived and prospered many years in Ghana, though not without faltering. After a bankruptcy, he and his partners picked themselves up and rebuilt the company. Like thousands of other British people who travelled abroad to work, our family history contains the ambiguity common to many expatriates. Are they still bearing a Scottish standard, or are they essentially changed by the colonial experience?

Grampa William's children, my father included, often did not see him for several years, but when he did take the steamship home, he would bring various unusual pets. So, in fairly obvious ways, my grandfather's returns from Africa made the family a bit exotic compared to its neighbours.

On one home trip, a spider monkey accompanied him. Family history does not tell if his pet enjoyed steerage-class accommodation, or was treated to more luxurious surroundings in cabin class. Did it read the Bible with Grampa and pass comment on its ancestor's place in Noah's Ark? Perhaps it became accustomed to superior treatment, but back in Glasgow the spider monkey was scolded and punished for some deed, and it scampered away and up to a ledge quite high on the wall, about 6 to 8 feet above ground where special assiettes and other plates were kept, either for display or storage. With simian humour the monkey exacted revenge for his scolding, hurling these china plates one by one to the kitchen floor.

Dinner on board ship was usually a formal matter, with the men all in black ties, the ladies in full-length evening dresses. For Scotsmen, a kilt and Argyll black jacket can be a very formal outfit and Grampa did wear the kilt. Another of the pets he brought home was a chameleon. My imagination conjured up images of Grampa's chameleon, dressed for dinner. Presumably its tartan merged with the colour of the surroundings it chose at the time. I never knew the chameleon's name; it proved to be a much less interactive pet than the spider monkey, and in Glasgow lived in the greenhouse. Unfortunately, it tended to blend in all too well and seemed to be lost for weeks at a time, disguising itself as a tomato vine or a cucumber. Despite this, it did not seem to understand hunting in northern climes and began to wither away. So Grampa's sons used to purchase flies as chameleon dinner. Alas, the chameleon eventually escaped and they never saw it again.

A nearby neighbour, however, was an alcoholic and as he crawled home one night on all fours, he came face to face with a dragon. Its eyes came out on stalks, he said, and swivelled independently to assimilate the humanoid before it. Whether it spat fire, we do not know, but the neighbours whispered that he was suffering from the DT's (delirium tremens). He swore off drink for good.

The most exotic of Grampa's travel companions was a chimpanzee. Given the large size of my own ears, plus my long arms, some family remarked that Grampa William had surely just found and adopted his grandson from a troop of local Ghanaian chimps.

They Called Me Otherwise

Equa was a female and became quite the companion. According to family legend retold by my father, she would greet Grampa when he came home from work, untie his shoes and bring him his slippers. For this simple deed she was rewarded with an after-dinner cigar. She and Grampa would sit on either side of the hearth, having a good old puff. Now Grampa liked only the best (and that meant Cuban) cigars. I often wonder if his generosity extended to giving Equa his Cuban cigars. Maybe she was fobbed off with ersatz fakes.

Equa grew too powerful for the Glasgow home and so she was given to the Edinburgh Zoo. With our present knowledge it was an unkind fate. She was mated and produced a baby, but lacked parenting skills. She became unstable and her keepers were terrified of her. On a return from Africa, Grampa insisted on visiting his former companion. For his own safety, the zookeepers were just as adamant that they could not permit it. Grampa was a persuasive man, however, and indeed entered the cage by himself. Equa took one look at him, picked up her baby and brought it to Grampa, who cradled it in his arms. I do not know what became of Equa, nor her baby, but I cannot imagine that they survived much longer. It is a tragic story, but comic too.

Criminal Connections

In Accra, capital of Ghana, Grampa's position as a partner in the construction firm gained him membership in the colonial club for British expatriates and government civil servants posted abroad. Some of Grampa's fellow club members would have been to famous schools such as Eton, Harrow, Winchester, Fettes and probably Strathallan, where wee Wullie (that's me) was himself sent scores of years later.

The British at home have always been labelled as relatively class conscious. Their schools perpetuated the system, so that the term "old boy's network" is now understood to mean looking out for the "chaps who were at school with me." Fee-paying schools are confusingly called "public schools" in the U.K., whereas they are labelled private schools elsewhere. The point is that the parents pay, and the higher the fees, the more advantage this confers on the pupil in his later career.

Even in the colonies, the off-duty uniform of these men often included a blazer with an old-school crest embroidered on the breast pocket. Grampa William was a grand fellow, generous and successful at his career as architect and builder, but he didn't have that old-school connection. His qualifications had been earned the hard way, with a spade and a trowel, not with a silver spoon. But he did have that dry Scottish sense of humour, and it helped him put matters of old-school ties and blazers in perspective.

The colonial experience sometimes brought people of Britain's different social strata together. Identification with the old country gave them fellowship with those who, back on the home turf, would not have been their associates. Grandfather felt he had to have an embroidered blazer badge, and he had an exquisite one made up. "One had to keep one's end up at the club," as the colonial saying was, and he did have a panache about him, did William. An acquaintance noticed him and his new blazer with crest, on arrival at the club. According to my father, the conversation proceeded thus.

"Galloway, I say, what a striking badge. What school did you attend, dear chap?"

Close examination revealed the badge had four quadrants, each with a suitable emblem. One had a ball and chain, another had prison-cell bars; a third depicted a pair of shovels, and in the fourth quadrant was a hangman's noose. The motto, "Adsum 'ard labor," suited a famous reform school for delinquent adolescents.

"I was at Borstal. Did you not know?" replied Grampa. The colonial was speechless.

My grandfather's returns home to Scotland were always a cause for great family excitement. Like so many of his fellow British members of Accra society, Grampa reached to his Glasgow home for renewal. One needed to have one's

Scottishness topped up, as I found out myself later. It wasn't easy to leave one's family and travel to Africa for extended periods. Grandfather would sail from Accra to Liverpool on the Elder Dempster Line, and would spend usually several months back in Glasgow becoming reacquainted with his family. He would regale his listeners with stories, sometimes tall, sometimes true, from darkest Africa.

All too soon after a respite in Glasgow, however, he had to return to his work, and on the eve of sailing back to West Africa, a gloom could be seen settling over the family. I became acquainted with that same sadness upon returning to boarding school, and at airports and docksides throughout our history as family left Johannesburg, or Glasgow, or London or Vancouver. It was worse in the days when travel took longer and other communications were much slower, but the Galloway diaspora has been a constant in our lives.

Grandfather always held a party on the eve of his journey back to Accra. It was the occasion to see friends before he left, and it also gave the family a focus, an activity, before they had to say goodbye to him. On one such occasion, a long-standing friend came over and remarked, "Willie, you've a glum look on your face. Is there something on your mind, man? We've been longtime friends, and you can tell me if there's something bothering you."

Granddad looked his friend in the eye, then bent his head closer, in conspiracy. "Matt, you'll understand that there are some things not spoken in the family. It's a terrible shame, and there's not many know; but you've been a good friend to me these years. I just can't help thinking about my own brother. It's ten years to the day since he was hanged for murder."

When I was pursuing family genealogy recently, I found in the 1901 official Census for Glasgow a younger brother of said William. Nobody in the family had ever mentioned this sibling. He was nineteen at census time, living at Overnewton

Square in Glasgow. Neither have any subsequent records been unearthed. So does the family perhaps have a mysterious skeleton, a scandal after all?

These stories of his chimp companion, of poking fun at the stiff British civil servants, were told to me as factual, but we also know that my grandfather was a great raconteur and storyteller. Maybe they did not happen exactly as told. Perhaps the narrators were testing me to see if I accepted them as a literal truth. Perhaps I came to realise that they convey much of my grandfather's style, whether factually exact or exaggerated. They are corroborated by other family members, but perhaps ultimately their source was the same as mine, so I do not know.

Hooch Mon

Today, we could not easily import chimpanzees, spider monkeys and chameleons from West Africa to Britain. Governments impose all sorts of barriers. In the case of animal export, the restrictions are in the best interests of the species. For some other products, the limits merely serve government interests, as my family has often discovered.

Grandfather's son David, my uncle, had emigrated to the United States sometime before the 1929 Depression. Granny visited her son in the U.S. only once. While there, she saw a wristwatch that she wanted for her husband William, but she did not want to pay duties on returning to Scotland. She might have worn it and declared it, or thrown it in the bottom of her suitcase. All these would have been less incriminating than sewing a special watch-smuggling pouch into her corset. This was in the days before metal detectors were used on travellers. Fortunately, she was not challenged and she triumphed over the bureaucrats' need for tax revenue.

My father, much more innocent, had a different experience.

Criminal Connections

In 1930 he sailed for the U.S. at the age of nineteen to visit his brother David in Boston. Several older men were friendly to this Glaswegian youngster, playing deck games with him and showing interest in his career ambitions. He was studying classics at Glasgow University, with thoughts of becoming a minister. He certainly was a trusting person.

On the eve of docking, an American approached him and confessed that he had too much luggage, so perhaps the young man would help him by taking one of his cases. This was agreed. The man asked that they meet up just outside the customs shed, where he would retrieve the suitcase.

Once my father had disembarked from the ship, the customs officer asked him to open suitcase number one. Granny had heard that her second son, David, sorely missed his steak and kidney pie, and my father had been supplied with two pie funnels for his brother. A pie funnel collects water from the bottom of the pie dish, as it turns to steam, and releases it out the top, thereby preventing the pastry from becoming too soggy. A good steak and kidney pie could be four inches deep.

The customs officer rummaged around and produced the pie funnels. Puzzled, he demanded to know what they were. Pie, to an American, is a flatter dish, for example an apple pie, so explanations had to be given. Satisfied, the customs officer bade father a pleasant stay and sent him on.

Meeting his elder brother David, he explained that he had to hand over a suitcase to a fellow passenger. David, being a bit more worldly, demanded to know what was in the case, but his younger sibling did not know. This was the time of Prohibition in the States, and also, my father was young and naïve. When they opened the suitcase, they found it was full of whisky. My father was a smuggler! Now David enjoyed a tipple himself, and he was outraged that anyone would take advantage of his younger brother and endanger him with imprisonment for smuggling booze. So he insisted that my

They Called Me Otherwise

father not keep his rendezvous with the real criminal. They would appropriate the whisky, leaving this lowlife to wait on his corner for his hooch.

Following this trip, perhaps understanding how naïve his view of the world had been, my father decided to become an accountant instead of a minister.

In keeping with the repeated family pattern of emigration, my father and mother sailed from Britain to South Africa immediately after their wedding in 1938, on the *Athlone Castle* of the Union Castle Shipping Line.

War broke out in 1939, so it wasn't until late 1946, after the troops had been repatriated, that my family was eventually able to return to Scotland for a visit. By this time, my parents had brought my sister into the world, born 1941. Grandfather William, also unable to get home during those war years, returned from Africa, so the family was finally able to celebrate a Scottish Hogmanay together in Glasgow, the first in nine years. I was to be born nine months later.

Although suffering ill health at that time, my grandfather, on learning of my beginnings in 1947, was delighted at the prospect of another grandchild and pronounced that I would be a boy. My parents and elder sister bade farewell to Grampa and Granny, and sailed back to South Africa in early 1947 with me as a passenger in utero.

On Good Friday, April 4, 1947 my grandfather was reading his Bible, as presumably a good Presbyterian Christian should do on that solemn day. He looked up from his reading and remarked to his wife, "You know, Kate, there's much humour in the Bible."

She asked back, "Aye, Willie, you'll be giving me an example?" but she received no response. Granddad William was dead....

I was born in October 1947, a boy, as grandfather had insisted. Of course I was named William. I never met this man, but from the stories told about him, it is obvious that he was a larger-than-life person. He was sorely missed when he died. He had spent so much of his life abroad, and was cheated of a time to savour his retirement back in Glasgow. The fact that his stories lived on after him is an indication of how big a person he was in our lives. The family torches have passed to his children and in turn to his grandchildren, including me. It was expected that we should be great contributors.

I personally had nagging doubts. As a boy, Wullie lacked that essential ingredient for boyhood success, namely proficiency in sports. It seemed Wullie wasn't too bright either, but eventually I found that label to be untrue. This is a story of growth, in that particularly Scottish way of using what ingredients you have and making do with them.

This then, is the story of a Scots lad: my experiences, failures, triumphs, travels, friendships and some encounters with food and wine. The book started as a series of episodes, but extended into a journey in life. The stories initially seemed to be unconnected, but on examination, they really are an expression of a Scottish personality in a boy called Wullie. It is in some ways a tale of redemption.

CHAPTER TWO

Easy Living
Johannesburg 1947 to 1958

Manners? Bananas?

My father, mother and sister had returned home to South Africa after that grand Christmas holiday reunion in Scotland, 1946. My 1947 birth was not marked by difficulty and we grew together, a family of four, in the Johannesburg suburb of Saxonwold. Being not far from the zoo, we could honestly say to our family in Scotland that we could often hear the African lions roaring nearby. We were perfectly safe from predators, of course. There were no great traumas for me to endure in the first few years of life. I was not likely to be lion dinner. British food rationing during and post World War II was unknown in South Africa. The family was relatively prosperous.

As a young child, I was not initially conscious that the Apartheid system of South Africa was strange. Awareness came gradually over many years, not from one event. The African summers were warm, even hot, and the winters, although chilly, did not grind one down in the same way that Glasgow winters could. Life was more opulent in Johannesburg than it could have been in Glasgow, and relied a bit more on glitz than on self-directed humour. So there was not a great

Easy Living: Johannesburg

incentive among white South Africans to question the source of their prosperity too deeply.

My family was liberal and tolerant for its time, and my father's Scottish sense of humour was an ever present feature in the family, if not in the wider African society. On one occasion he was admonishing me and probably about to administer corporal punishment. He was about to ask where were my manners, but his eye caught one of those elongated yellow fruits and he slipped: "Wullie, where are your bananas?"

Manners were forever called bananas after that....

In all, from my conception in Glasgow, birth in Johannesburg and to the age of eight, I made at least four trips between Scotland and South Africa. A well travelled boy, I recall flying on KLM Royal Dutch Airlines' Super Constellation planes, landing en route in Brazzaville, Kano or Khartoum.

Plenty of Peaches and Plums

Being such a comfort to most of us, food has a capacity to evoke long reminiscences. I have always enjoyed good food and the memories surrounding the good company of friends and family participating in meals together.

A particular scene is embedded in my mind from Christmas 1951. Our South African garden was laden with peaches and plums, it being summer in the southern hemisphere. We were to fly to Scotland for Christmas and we packed a suitcase full of fruit. It was so very welcome in Scotland, where postwar rationing still ruled. I was personally forbidden to eat any while we were there. South Africa was a land of plenty, a contrast to our beloved Glasgow. The Scottish city may have been drab in its grey winter coat, but the family connection was warm and cheerful.

On the eve of a subsequent holiday I was unwell, and my

parents feared I would not be fit to travel to Scotland. They bundled me off to bed, and gave me a cartoon book to peruse. It was my first introduction to the Oor Wullie character. Whatever influences he may have had, I was remarkably fit the following day and the trip was not postponed. As a bonus I became more attuned to the Glasgow accents, which I was about to encounter again.

Johannesburg is a city whose wealth flows from gold mining. If it made my family more prosperous than they could have been in Glasgow, it also demanded that we acknowledge the source of the gold, the engine that powered our journeys back to Scotland.

Gold on Them Thar Tables

At about eight years of age, I went down a gold mine, Blyvooruitzicht. This educational experience was organised by Father, possibly just for interest, but likely because he had a sense of exposing his children to new things and showing them that, professional accountant family though we might be, we were only a few thousand feet from miners.

The first problem was that all the helmets were made for adult heads. Wullie's head was still disproportionately small compared to his body (many prehistoric creatures suffer from this indignity). So when the light was hooked onto the helmet, the whole contraption fell across his face, making it impossible to see anything. The light had to be carried.

The visitors entered a cage elevator. Outside, an overseer latched the iron grid gate closed with a huge bar and then sounded a klaxon. We began our descent, about 1,000 metres or more, clanking as we proceeded. Once underground it was much hotter than one might have expected; the visitors didn't walk far, but took a train to the gold face. Wullie was even

Easy Living: Johannesburg

seated in the lap of a burly miner, who played the charade of making him feel that he was actually drilling.

Later, lunch was served—the same as the miners ate, though more delicately presented. After that, there was a tour to see gold ore being crushed and smelted. Finally the party was ushered into a locked room, with protective iron bars all around. A solitary ingot of gold sat on the table, and it weighed about 70 pounds. Gold was priced at $35, or £7, per ounce in those days, so for sixteen ounces to the pound, this represented almost $40,000. One could purchase many chocolate bars for such a sum, thought the boy Wullie. The gold bar positively beckoned to all the visitors. When another guest asked the weight, the tour guide jokingly offered that if the person could lift the bar with one hand and raise it above his head, he could take it away. Needless to say, at eight years old Wullie could only fantasise at being such a hero. The opportunity would never come again—would it?

Wullie dreamed of succeeding at this task. A family friend, who was both muscular and had bushy eyebrows was asked for the secret to his strength. Was he, like Samson in the Bible, strong only when he was hairy? The friend advised, with all solemnity, that eating chicken skin was the secret to being strong and having bushy eyebrows. So Wullie began eating chicken skin. The denouement occurred in my late teenage years, though my eyebrows never became bushy.

Joking with Uncle Jimmy

Like my grandfather, we travelled back home to reaffirm our Eurocentric natures, not quite able to sever the strings and become South Africans. On several trips between 1950 and 1958, I was able to meet my lovely Uncle Jimmy. He was a cheerful man with a pawky sense of humour; resourceful too.

A bank manager with the Bank of Scotland, Uncle Jimmy arrived one morning to find that they could not get into the bank for some reason. A queue of customers wished to withdraw funds and to deposit. With a little organisation, he took deposits from his car window, kept a transaction ledger and he paid out the same cash, plus whatever he had personally, to customers who wished to withdraw a pound or two. He continued until the bank could be properly opened.

Improvisation like that is a skill required of good actors, and Uncle Jimmy might have been in the theatre, so adept were his talents at mimicry, impersonations, manner affectation and disguise. He would put on an old hat, pull a grubby scarf around his neck and slip out the door. Soon he would ring his doorbell, and Aunt Patricia would go to open the portal.

"Mussus," Jimmy would mutter. "Mussus, could you spare a tanner for the poor (pronounced as Glaswegians do, more like "puir"). Ah've a wife at hame and a wean. We're no' asking much, just enough for a bit tae eat."

"Away home with you," Pat would intone. "We've not much to spare. My husband is generous and gives at his office. We've a child ourselves, too."

"But, mussus, we're awfy short; could you just manage a thruppenny bit for a poke of chips?" bargained Jimmy, lowering his price to half his original tanner.

"No, we can't. Now away with you."

"Would your husband turn away a man like me?"

Patricia was becoming quite agitated by the tramp's insistence. It was time to call for reinforcements. "Jimmy!" she called back into the house. Jimmy didn't seem to hear her. "JIMMY!" she cried out again. By this time, the "tramp" could contain his mirth no longer and a snort of laughter erupted from behind the scarf. A startled Patricia looked closer.

"Jimmy!" she yelled, "That's not fair." She'd chase him back into the house, and try to browbeat him into admitting that he was naughty. Patricia had a lovely sense of humour herself too, so could always appreciate the funny side, once she recovered.

On another occasion, Patricia needed to repair a nightgown. It was warm in the parlour, and she slipped it off to perform the darn. There was a ring at the doorbell, and she froze. Who might be visiting at such an hour? The front door was heard to open and she caught Jimmy's voice. "Good evening, Mr. Dunbar. How kind of you to call. Mrs. Whyte is in the parlour. Please come in. You'll have a cup of tea?" Mr. Dunbar was the name of their local church minister.

"Jimmy, no! Jimmy, you can't come in here. JIMMY! Jimmy, I'm not decent."

Jimmy didn't heed Patricia's plaintive call and the door to the parlour opened. Jimmy ushered in an invisible man.

Yet another time, when Patricia was in the parlour after a long day, she heard the doorbell ring and Jimmy answered it. "Come in, Mr. Dunbar. How kind of you to call. Mrs. Whyte is in the parlour."

"Och, havers, Jimmy. You tricked me like that once before. That windbag wouldn't call so late in the evening." The door opened; the minister himself entered the room.

One Saturday morning, Jimmy wanted to see about some knocking sound coming from underneath the car. Patricia went out for a while shopping and on returning home saw the feet protruding out from underneath the vehicle. Upon passing, she leaned over and affectionately tickled the body. The head came up swiftly, bumped itself on the car and abruptly went down again. Meanwhile Patricia went into the kitchen, where Jimmy was boiling the kettle for a cup of tea. Before she could grasp the confusion of seeing him there, Jimmy said, "Did you see our friend Robert underneath the car when you came by? He was passing and since he knows a lot about cars, I asked him to have a look at ours."

At that moment, Robert staggered into the kitchen, bruised on the head and, I'm sure, surprised by the display of unexpected affection.

Christmas Dinner for a Stranger

Although we had returned to Scotland for Christmas holidays three or four times in a decade, on the other years we would celebrate Christmas in the southern hemisphere summer, with the usual hot turkey meal, presents, carol singing and reindeer decorations. My mother, always the gracious and hospitable hostess, invited others who did not have wide circles of family and friends. Father was working one Christmas Eve, about to close the office. He was senior partner with the chartered accountant firm of Alex Aiken and Carter (now part of KPMG's empire; KPMG [Klynveld Peat Marwick Goerdeler] is one of the large accounting firms worldwide today). Miss Springate, his secretary, entered to announce that a gentleman had arrived at the office and although he did not have an appointment, wished to see a senior partner right away.

The man was ushered in and lost no time with pleasantries. "I own a shipping outfit. I'm here from England for a few days. Need you to draw up articles of incorporation for a new company right away."

Christmas in South Africa is summer time, so it is usual for offices to close for more than just a couple of days. Father explained that the office would reopen on the second of January, and he would then immediately draw up the requisite papers. The office was already quiet, with only a few staff left. Despite the summer season, by British tradition, incongruously they had snowmen, sleigh bells and holly in the office—but the visitor was not interested in the trappings of Christmas.

"No, no. I intend to float the company today, before Christmas and certainly before the New Year." The cornered senior partner, my father, protested that the office was really about to close, but the shipping magnate, Eric by name, dismissed the plea.

"Do you want the business? If so, we conduct it today."

So the senior partner's wife, my mother, was telephoned and the explanation given that my father would be late that night, not early. "You say the man is from England? What is he doing for Christmas?" Father did not know and less did he care. A diet of cold congealed mopani worms would be too good a Christmas fare for this interloper. "You must invite him for Christmas dinner; he's a stranger far from home." Father argued, but his good wife had the last word, so Eric was curtly invited to lunch, which he courteously accepted.

It turned out that Eric really was a shipping tycoon. He visited the family several times afterwards and was especially kind to the wee Wullie, advising him seriously on how to outfit the plank of wood he called his boat to make it a luxurious yacht. (Eric owned a yacht, complete with crew).

Just Missing the Royal Connection

At this age, I was interested in electric trains as well as toy yachts. Apparently Prince Charles, of a similar age to myself, had a Hornby Dublo—the same kind that my father bought for me. Of all my toys, this provided the most fun and fascination. We made scenery out of chicken wire with cotton batting soaked in plaster covering. Suitably painted, it looked realistic through my child's eyes. We had lights and a village church. The station even had people waiting, and a porter with luggage. Wullie wondered if Prince Charles had a grander setup than he did. Perhaps some time, while our family was in the U.K., he'd invite Wullie over to play one afternoon.

At the age of ten, I was to be sent to boarding school in Scotland. This strange ritual was common in some families at the time. It was the done thing—"make a man of him, you'll see"—so I was entered for Gordonstoun and provisionally accepted. Gordonstoun is a school in the Highlands of Scotland, then run by a Dr. Hahn. His philosophy was a very Outward Bound one, with emphasis on outdoor activities. He taught boys how to develop trust and reliance on each other, in a physically challenging environment. I had visions of boys with crampons, rope and tackle ascending local mountains. I was saved from this fate because Father's sister, my Aunt Nan, drove up from Glasgow to visit the school, and immediately wrote back that under no circumstances should I attend Gordonstoun, since I was a more studious personality. Prince Charles was eventually sent there, but I was destined to go to Strathallan in Perthshire instead, and so Prince Charles never had the opportunity to meet Wullie and find out that they both had the same kind of electric train.

Oor Wullie and The Telly

To be admitted to such a school, Wullie had to pass the "Eleven-plus" exam, so named because it was administered to children age eleven. To pass would enable entry to grammar school, and also to what the British confusingly call "public school" (the likes of Strathallan). To fail the exam at this tender age was to be streamed to a less academic schooling.

To set a high standard is admirable. To penalise all who could not jump that high at that age was reprehensible. Wullie had no say in the matter; his eleven-plus exam was scheduled, but the problem was that he had only just turned ten. Wullie sat this exam while still in South Africa, one Saturday morning, under the watchful eye of his grade four maths teacher.

The first question on the exam asked what was a cathode-ray tube. Bear in mind that South Africa did not have television at all in 1958. My father, after reading the exam paper later, realised that his wee Wullie could not possibly know that answer.

Easy Living: Johannesburg

"Of course I know what a cathode-ray tube is!" Wullie shot back. "Oor Wullie in the *Sunday Post* thought he could build a telly, and he read about cathode-ray tubes and pulse synchronisation from a library book." Kudos to that high-class comic, Oor Wullie.

It had been a mistake that Wullie should pass an exam which he had been expected to fail. This infamous Eleven-plus exam from Britain had been administered only for practice, so that he might do well or adequately well the following year when he would be eleven. Alas, Wullie had failed to fail and so had passed!

Wullie, almost eleven, ready for Strathallan

CHAPTER THREE

My Early Education about Birds and Bees
Scotland 1958 to 1960

Giving up Oor Wullie and South Africa

Thus did Oor Wullie help me both into Scottish society and also specifically into my school. Although he had been a pre-teenage boy for well over half a century, I did not have that luxury and was forced to leave my antihero behind as I was hurled into the adult world. So although I owe a deep gratitude to the Wullie character in making me what I am, it was necessary for me to leave him behind to his eternal boyhood. I am forever grateful for his guidance and influence, and he does appear again occasionally to check up on me as an adult.

But these are my stories and I cannot blame him for my foibles or personality any more. Some essentials remain, for that is what constitutes a personality. Like the cartoon character, I make do with what I have and enjoy life very much that way.

My father and I left the comfort of South Africa in August 1958, sailing to Southampton and then taking the *Royal Scotsman* train up North. This was no holiday trip. This was physical and cultural removal, a dress rehearsal for becoming a grown-up. My father had decided that we should go to live in Scotland, his main reason being uncertainty about the future of South Africa, given its increasingly right-wing government. He and I were the advance party, with my mother and sister to follow a few months later. Up until that time, we had oscillated between Scotland and South Africa, living in Johannesburg, but maintaining the Scottish link with our frequent holidays. Now we were abandoning South Africa and making Scotland our home base.

Strathallan: One Question Too Many

On a bright 1958 September afternoon, in a uniform several sizes larger than my slight frame required, I stood forlornly watching Father and my Aunt Nan's husband, Uncle Clifford, drive away down the tree-lined avenue close to Riley House. I had been deposited at boarding school. I was still ten years old, although when asked my age, would always say "almost eleven," as children need to aspire. I was in a class where some boys were already twelve. These hulking fellows, in some cases, had deeper voices, broader shoulders and were teaching themselves how to swagger. This they did by swinging their arms more widely and attempting to walk as if bow-legged. It was intended to give the impression of bulk.

Indeed, within less than a year, several boys had fallen over that precipice called puberty, though not our Wullie of course. I remained ignorant of the changes about to assault my body, and the devil's tricks that accompany this ascent to the depths of heaven and plunge to the heights of purgatory.

Mr. B. was an extraordinarily excellent science teacher. He knew his discipline well and brought a real scientific objectivity to the classroom, not encumbered by the petty minds of small boys. The class came at last to the issue of reproduction—in worms only, of course. Worms are hermaphrodites and when

My Early Education About Birds & Bees

they produce eggs, they lie in the "69" position. Laws that prohibit this among people in certain states of America, apparently, do not apply to earthworms. The egg is produced and it rolls down the groove between their backs, to fall on the ground.

Mr. B. cleared his throat several times before embarking on the delicate matter of worm reproduction and finally said, "Well, we all know how reproduction occurs in the human species, but, er, worms are hermaphrodites and eggs are produced in an, er, entirely different, er, manner." There was a waving of a hand in the air, which Mr. B. tried not to notice. This pesky boy, however, would not give up and finally he had to interrupt the rolling egg in mid-ecstasy. "What is it, boy?"

Wullie clearly asked, "Please, Surr, I don't know how reproduction is done in humans, Surr."

The science master shook slightly, as the earth trembles a warning before an earthquake. There was a sudden stillness and the birds outside ceased to sing.

"How dare you! How dare you! You insolent boy!" roared Mr. B. "I shall report you to your housemaster for this. You'll be flogged!" There were sniggering guffaws all around at the temerity and brazen insubordination, particularly because they came from that wee Wullie who seemed so innocent and was not usually troublesome in class. Yet Wullie had not the merest clue as to what he had done.

Later in the day, around prep, the housemaster, Mr. Hewson, called him to his study. "You were disruptive in Mr. B's class today?"

"No Surr?"

"Perhaps you could tell me exactly what was said?"

The episode was innocently retold, to the best of Wullie's memory. If Mr. Hewson smiled, he did so only inside, but he must have understood exactly what had happened.

"Perhaps you could contain your exuberance for questions in Mr. B.'s class."

There wasn't any explanation of what Wullie had not understood. It took a year longer before the awful truth dawned and I saw just how Wullie's question had been misconceived. Some who know me would grin, thinking that in my adult years I still didn't always seem to be quite "in touch."

Forever Naïve

Another example of innocence, aged eleven. Wullie accompanied his parents to a movie called *The French Mistress*, in which a young French teacher arrives at an all-boys boarding school (the sort that Wullie himself attended). The headmaster's son, also a teacher, falls for the new glamorous enseignante, but his father forbids the alliance, saying that he had himself known the young lady's mother.

After the movie, Wullie grilled the parents. Why would the fact that the father (and headmaster) had known the young teacher's mother mean that the son could not become romantically attached? My parents tried to explain—in general terms. I sensed the people in the next row being mightily amused at their predicament. The more they dwelt upon generalities, the more did Wullie press them for specifics, much to their embarrassment. Wullie was still in that Garden of Eden state of not having eaten of the tree of knowledge—and he did not learn the truth that night, but his parents' discomfort lives on in his mind.

No, "the truth" came in a more prosaic form. Wullie built model boats and aeroplanes. In one of these, the instructions said to join the stand's male part to the female part and glue firmly together. Now Wullie was not quick, but even he could figure out that the male stand had a protuberance, whereas the female stand had an—uh, well, uh—you get the point. One and one made two, and so Wullie deduced the birds and the bees from model aeroplane stands.

My Early Education About Birds & Bees

Later, as an adult in Collins Bay prison for hardened criminals, this fine understanding of sex education, as taught to me by Wullie, was to serve me well.

Waxworks Handshake

A little before that episode, just after Christmas 1958, my father and I took the train down to London to meet my mother and sister, at last joining us from South Africa. I had just completed my first term at Strathallan boarding school and had a couple of weeks' respite from the rigours of school. My mother and sister had stayed on in South Africa because my sister's school year ended in December, and she was finishing up her important final year of senior school.

On the eve of their ship's arrival in the Port of London I was excited, anticipating seeing my mother and sister again after a four-month separation. My father needed a diversion to stop me asking how long until the ship docked, so took me to Madame Tussauds famous waxworks in London to help pass the hours. It turned out that Santa Claus was there that day and my dad told me to go over and shake his hand. Unwittingly I did, only to discover that this Santa was wax, though obviously very realistic.

Embarrassed, I failed to notice a Canadian girl, about a year younger than myself, also visiting the museum. Her father, a zoology professor at the University of British Columbia in Vancouver, was on sabbatical at Oxford and their family was also enjoying London attractions. I had only just turned eleven in October, so didn't pay much attention to girls, at least not then. I had to go back to Africa and then return to Scotland eleven years later, before this girl's presence would become significant.

School Food: A Doggy Delicacy

In a few hours I was reunited with my mother and sister. But all too soon, after a brief Christmas break, I was sent back to school, to endure the second term and to suffer the institutional food. It was, to my sensitive nature, quite simply revolting. On arrival that first day of the first term at boarding school at the age of ten, I had enjoyed a sumptuous afternoon tea, with cakes and biscuits, scones and pancakes. Father offered the opinion that this was probably not the usual fare. Parents having departed, the diet in Scotland became porridge for breakfast. I could not stand the slimy stuff with lumps. So out of my three shillings pocket money per week, I purchased cereal from the tuck shop.

Steaks were never on the menu, but one day there appeared small, sausage-shaped slivers of meat in a breadcrumb coat. They tasted not too bad, so all the boys asked for the "ordinary helping." The choices were either "small helping" or "ordinary helping," but whichever was ordered, all the food on the plate had to be levered down the gorge before we could be dismissed from the meal.

These tasty morsels appeared occasionally on the menu. One clever wag said that they were dog, and so they became known. Some of us younger, more gullible boys assumed that we were eating dog, and whenever it appeared there would be yelps of "Dog? All ordinaries, please."

One day another tasty-looking treat arrived at the table. The steaming cauldrons appeared to contain chicken à la king—that is, chicken served in a white sauce. It had never been detected on the boarding-school radar before so all boys wanted ordinary, not small helpings.

Ah, what painful deception! What mean-spirited, conniving treachery by the kitchen staff! The solid bits in the mixture were not chicken but tripe. For those who know not tripe, it is bovine stomach lining—very tough, extremely impervious and rather like solid rubber, though not as flavourful.

Chew as we all did, the tripe did not yield or soften under our molars. After a considerable period, the allotted lunch time was running short and we had to swallow the mess whole. We had all wanted non-small portions and now we had to clean our plates.

All that glisters is not gold.

Strawberries and Cream

Boarding school in Scotland was a huge contrast to early life in South Africa. Wullie's introduction to rugby is still completely fresh in his brain today. The field had been used all summer to graze the sheep and cows. Your imagination of the gifts they left for the boys is accurate, though probably incomplete. Well fertilised, the ground also pushed up thousands of thistles, the hardy Scottish national plant. So not only could boys land in a pile of you know what, but they might also slide into a prickly thistle.

As the smallest, youngest, most bewildered creature of that year, Wullie frequently found himself at the bottom of the rugby scrum, with his face pushed well into the mud. Although allowed clean rugby clothes more frequently than once a term, Wullie did not understand this. It didn't take long before his rugby clothes assumed a life and a certain rigour of their own.

The first term had begun with relatively mild September temperatures. Then winter came, and in the month of February the temperature did not rise above 26 degrees Fahrenheit (about -3 Celsius). Boys were not permitted socks or hot water bottles or any such comforts in bed. Chilblains on fingers and toes were a constant winter agony. So it was all misery, right? Not at all.

Summer followed, and the well fertilised school fields produced a crop of strawberries. Boys were permitted to buy them for two shillings a pound punnet, which was an unbelievably good price even in those days. That's ten pence in sterling currency today, or about twenty-five cents Canadian. With his cereal money in hand, Wullie walked down to the school farm, where the farmer's wife took pity on this bedraggled ragamuffin and promptly piled some extra berries on top. It must have been a pound and a half. "Och, they're past their best. We'll only charge you a shilling," she said. Wullie thought they were still superb, but her parting words were the best, "Laddie, I'll bet you haven't had a chocolate biscuit in a wee while." It was true, and she sat Wullie down to tea and biscuits, heaped strawberries and cream.

Parents were kind enough to send supplementary food parcels, which were permitted three times per term. Cakes, biscuits and sweeties (candy, to North Americans) were prohibited contents. So the usual parcel had a couple of apples, a box of dates or raisins and perhaps a can of nuts. I also enjoyed the comics, especially the Scottish *Sunday Post*'s, with the cartoons of my hero, Oor Wullie. Unfortunately, cartoons were deemed to corrupt the boys' artistic potential and they were, therefore, on the forbidden list. There is also the possibility that hungry boys might have eaten the comics.

A couple of weeks after my twelfth birthday, October 1959, I received a tuck parcel from my parents. The housemaster inspecting my parcel did not notice that my apples were wrapped in Oor Wullie newspaper cartoons. The story line told of how Oor Wullie had himself hidden some sweeties away from his prying friends, in the barrels of two toy revolvers. How deliciously appropriate. My mother knew that I appreciated the humour of the comic character, and that I would understand the piquant relevance of this particular episode.

My Early Education About Birds & Bees

Lost In The Fog

At Christmas 1959, when I was paroled from school for holidays, the family was expecting a South African guest, Tessa. She was flying up from London just to visit for a day. We rose early to fetch Tessa at Edinburgh Airport, where she had elected to land rather than Glasgow, even though the latter was much closer. In the arrival area thousands of Scots were engaged in a pushing and shoving which resembled a rugby scrum, all trying to get to the front where they could see the arriving passengers.

It is said that airport arrival areas (I refuse to call them lounges) are deliberately made inhospitable, to discourage people from making a Sunday outing to see aeroplanes as a distraction from the rain. At last Tessa came through and we fought our way to join the queue (to the queue) to the car park. By this time the proverbial Scots mist was descending, and also it was already an hour later than we had intended it to be.

The journey to Glasgow, even before the motorway was built, was not that long. As the fog settled in, however, the traffic pace became more and more like waiting for one's income tax refund. The family had planned a trip around Loch Lomond but, by the time we arrived home in Glasgow the Sunday roast of beef was beginning to resemble black pudding. It was hurriedly served, since the time was already past two in the afternoon—four hours had elapsed since airport arrival.

Now the return flight was due to depart at 7:00 p.m., with check-in at 6:00 p.m. For us punctual Galloways, a command to present oneself for check-in for an event as important as an airline flight was like a royal summons to lunch. Given that it had taken over two hours to get home from Edinburgh airport, there was nothing else to do but re-embark in the grumbling Wolseley automobile and immediately repair to the airport. The fog by this time was serious, even by pea-soup standards.

They Called Me Otherwise

Progress was painfully slow and we craned our necks out the windows attempting to see anything through the ghostly shrouds. Not surprisingly, we were lost, so we stopped to ask directions of a Scot who was delicately tottering home.

"Weel, ye go doon the road an' ye tak the furst traffic lights an' turrn right; ye go on aboot a half mile. No, no ye go on tae the second traffic lights an' turrn right; aboot a mile or two ye'll come to a fork in the road; if ye tak the left one, ye've gone wrong. Ah, no, perhaps ye'd better go the way I mentioned at first. Doon tae the furst lights an' turn left, I mean right, an' ye might see the polis station, but then on a nicht like this ye might not."

"Do you mean turn left or turn right?" queried Mother.

"Aye, that's right, ye turn left at the second traffic light . . . "

Before this man so versed in the nuances of local cartography could enlighten us further, we thanked him profusely and drove on, anxiously. The time was 5:30 in the afternoon. It did not occur to us that if we were encountering difficulty in meeting the 6:00 p.m. check-in time, then so probably were all would-be passengers. It was by now completely dark as well as foggy, and progress was so slow that Mother stepped from the car and began to walk a few yards ahead, beckoning us to follow. She remarked uncertainly, "I don't think we're on the main road. There is grass growing up between the tyre tracks here."

Sure enough, we were on some farm track, completely off the road system and could hardly proceed, but presently Mother saw a wee light from a small hut. She walked over to it and knocked on the door. It was indeed a surprise to have a uniformed man open the door, letting out a bright yellow light. Where were we, she asked? And how could we get to Edinburgh Airport?

"The airport? Madame, yer on the rrunway!"

We burst upon the Edinburgh departure lounge just in time to hear the announcement that due to fog, the flight was cancelled, but buses would transport the stranded passengers to Glasgow Airport, where it was clear.

CHAPTER FOUR

The Hopeless Athlete
South Africa 1961 to 1964

Another Big Upheaval

In 1960, while I was still a pupil at Strathallan, there were shots fired in South Africa at a place called Sharpeville. The victims were black; the perpetrators were panicked police. Deep, rumbling reverberations were heard around the world. The South African stock market plunged and with it, our family assets. Life had not been easy back in Scotland, so once again, the family went on the move and returned to live in South Africa at the end of 1960.

We had spent just 28 months in Scotland, so I was by now just thirteen. In hindsight, a move back to South Africa at that time seems like a jump into the fire. We went back partly for economic reasons, and also because somehow we had not become properly established in Scotland. In truth, the family was not happy and we thought that returning to South Africa and its familiar friends and lifestyle would solve that.

I left my boarding school in Perthshire, and we sailed for Cape Town on the Ellerman & Bucknall Line's *City of York*. She was a 13,000-tonne vessel, twin screw, with one stack. About 100 passengers sailed on her and the accommodation was pleasant. Passengers had, for example, not seawater but fresh water in which to bathe, a luxury taken for granted on cruise ships these days.

This move marked my second big upheaval in life, not only in country and culture, but also because I really did have to start growing up. At thirteen, I began to understand that South African government policies were at least controversial and probably wrong, but at that age one is not usually called to stand up for principles very much.

Commander Wullie

The captain on that voyage back to Africa was an entertaining man, and at times he would invite a group of children to his cabin, where he demonstrated magic tricks. He would roll a newspaper into a funnel and pour a glass of milk into it. Then he would rumple the paper into a ball, smooth it out and show that it was completely dry. Later he would shape it again into a funnel and pour the milk back into the glass. He kept a bunch of junior passengers amused for hours on that 14-day voyage from England to Cape Town.

One evening, there was a "horse race." Passengers were given horses' names and the race was to drink a pint of beer, eat two dry cracker biscuits and then blow up a balloon until it burst. Wullie wasn't sure how he'd handle the beer, but at the last minute Father realised the problem of a thirteen-year-old in the sauce, and kindly had the barman substitute a pint of lemonade. Aargh! It was fizzy (the beer, being British, was flat). Most men could open their throats and pour a pint down, without it touching their lips, particularly when crossing the equator. The Wullie horse came last.

The Ellerman & Bucknall Line provided paper coasters to put underneath their drinks glasses, suitably embossed with the company name and emblem. These coasters were made up of several thin layers of absorbent tissue, pressed together. One lunch time, the captain challenged Wullie.

"If you can separate a coaster into more than six layers, I'll buy you a drink."

A true Scot in more ways than one, Wullie worked away separating the tissue layers, as a biologist might with a scalpel on a delicate organism, and finally did have seven tissue layers. Wullie was determined to get that free drink and hastened to find the captain. The latter maintained, however, that it had been a trick assignment because he knew for a fact there were only six layers to the tissue-paper coaster.

Wullie was crestfallen; it besmirched his integrity. To this day I wonder if the issue might come up again. Perhaps if Wullie were to run for parliament, the matter might become public knowledge. "Local candidate blamed in coaster mat fraud." The part which really rankles is that to this day I know that Wullie successfully separated seven sheets.

One day the captain invited Wullie to the bridge. He explained the compass, the radar and how to steer a course. The wheel had a notch in the top spoke so that the helmsman always knew when the rudder was centred. Wullie was allowed to take the helm and watched as the compass showed that the ship drifted slightly off course. He was shown how to correct this and after a while really began to feel the vessel's pulse. Small deviations from the plotted course of 162 degrees were expected, and the compass always gave evidence, allowing for correction.

The helmsman slipped away, perhaps to have a cigarette. The captain had long since departed, so here was wee Wullie, age thirteen, at the helm of a passenger vessel, one thousand tonnes for each of his years, with only the sea around him.

Another ship appeared on the horizon, but Wullie knew from his geography courses that this vessel was at least nine miles away, so continued on. A crew member appeared on the bridge and suddenly took immediate charge. Wullie was unaware that ships should pass port to port (left side to left side), so vessels wanting to occupy the same railway lines on the ocean should both turn slightly to starboard (right). Alas it was too late for that. The other ship was well to the right of Wullie's ship, at the one o'clock position. To pass port to port would have required turning sharply to the right (starboard), so cutting across her bows and risking being rammed broadside. Wullie's ship turned instead hard to port, heading east in towards the African coast, and had to perform a long detour before resuming 162 degrees true, the intended south-southeast course.

Wullie was relieved of his command and has never since attempted to steer any waterborne vessel except a canal boat—at 2 knots.

Tortoise Rescues

No thanks to my navigation skills, we arrived safely back in Johannesburg in early 1961 and rented a flat in a suburb called Illovo ("the elephant place"). We were reasonably close to long-standing good friends, the Barrows, and my mother had an open invitation to swim in their pool any time.

The swimming pool area was surrounded by a wall, and inside this enclosure lived two tortoises; the larger one was about ten inches across its shell and quite aggressive. He was inclined (actually I never discovered the sex of this reptile, but chauvinistically assumed it was male) to nudge the smaller tortoise, which was a little more than half his size, around the pool edge until the poor, hapless, wretched, miserable creature fell in. At this stage, its terrapin ancestry asserted itself, and it would swim up and down. The pool, however, did not have a shallow incline suitable for tortoise landing, so after several hours this exhausted creature would sink.

Mrs. Barrow, with four sons and a daughter, usually had no difficulty in effecting a rescue. At times, nevertheless, they were all out and at this stage, plan B was set in motion: call 41-

0121 for my mother. She in turn alerted me, and I hastened to the Barrow home, bypassed the house, went straight to the change room, pulled on swimming trunks and prepared for the rescue.

There were no long lines to reel in by the lifeguard, nor flotation devices. I would plunge into the water, dive to the bottom and pick up the reptile, then bring it to the surface. Mouth-to-mouth resuscitation was never attempted, because the tortoise made it plain to me that such intimacy would not be appreciated. The tortoise would then be placed on dry land, far from the big bully—until the next time. It was an honour to serve the tortoise community thus, and I was justly proud of my rescue attempts.

I displayed a penchant for rescuing animals. Exhausted bees were sometimes given sugar water to give them energy sufficient to resume their flights. A lamb was rescued from the Leeds–Liverpool Canal. After all, I thought, what if humans sometimes reincarnated as amœbae?

Boys, Insects & Spiders

In late January of 1961, I was to continue my boarding-school life in the province of Natal, South Africa, and became reacquainted with several chums I had known up to the age of ten, when I had not failed the Eleven-plus exam. This school was 400 miles by train from our home city of Johannesburg, and in a beautiful setting. As the school brochures described it, "Nestled in the foothills of the Drakensberg Mountains...." We nicknamed it, sarcastically, "Happy Valley."

We called one boy "Grime" at school, because he was impervious to any washing. Even after a good scrub, Grime still looked as if, well, as if he needed a good scrub. Fine sand particles were etched behind his ears, and his knees always had that "fresh from the mucky rugby fields" look. Grime kept a live snake for a pet in his blazer pocket and he delighted in terrorising any non-herpetologists.

Most of us boys at term's end would board the train for an overnight trip home. Grime, of course, brought along his friend, but regrettably it escaped during the night on one of our journeys. Perhaps it had gone in search of some smaller boy to swallow. In truth, it was a grass snake, and they don't tend to find adolescent boys very tasty. The compartment door had been closed all night, as had the window. There was only one possible exit. It must have glided into the ventilation channel, which ran close to the top of each compartment. Grime searched to no avail. The boys disembarked to meet bewildered parents, who wondered what teenage monsters or reptiles were returning into their homes.

That should have been the story's end. Grime did not ever get this snake back. However, boys' imaginations fuelled marvellous tales. We envisioned the headmaster travelling by train. When the snake became hungry or thirsty, it would slink out and slither across the headmaster's face. This serpentine encounter would be revenge, or atonement, for the sins of many canings that the headmaster had hurled upon the bottoms of adolescent boys, trying to force them into a state of knowledge.

There were other encounters with wild life at school. Boys were permitted a long "lie" in bed on Sunday. It was certainly past 7:00 a.m. when Wullie gently roused. Glancing up at the wall above his bed, originally painted pale blue, he saw a huge spider about the size of his palm, with great hairy legs, hovering on the wall like a Black Hawk attack helicopter. A fellow schoolmate had been waiting. His socks were already curled into a grenade, which he hurled hard at the spider. It dropped onto Wullie's pillow.

Now all boys knew that these huge arachnids were actually harmless. As it landed, just inches from Wullie's face, instinct ruled over reason. Wullie leapt from his bed, threw the pillow

The Hopeless Athlete

to the floor, dislodging the spider. He slammed it with his pillow, then ground his shoe on top of it, so that there was only spider goo left. Some of its many legs were never found, such had been the fury of the attack against it.

I was then, and am now, ashamed of this brutal display against spiders. Of course the other bugs in the dormitory all laughed at my performance.

It was in fact a doubly cruel act because spiders were actually friends. Imagine, if you will, being a mosquito. For any species bent on survival, plentiful food is essential. Nowhere in the world could you find a more bounteous source of sweet blood than in a boys' boarding school. The mosquitoes were in paradise, living on those formerly blue walls. They groaned with delight each morning, replete, lazy and engorged. So any spider that would reduce the mosquito population was, on the "enemy's enemy" principle, really a friend.

Boys exacted their own vivid revenge on the mosquitoes. In the early morning, unable to move, with their bellies distended, mosquitoes could easily be squashed on the wall. A careful, quick boy could, with sang-froid, write part of his name in the liberated blood. Thus did the walls over time become less blue, with names of young red-blooded males.

Is The Moon Mendacious?

A couple of years earlier at boarding school in Scotland, I had encountered Mr. Hewson, who was a fund of anecdotes and mnemonics to assist in learning Latin. "*Domus domorum* commonly; bear locative *domi* in mind, the rest like *gradus* is declined" helped one remember how to decline the Latin noun *domus*, the word for home.

One evening when the moon was shining he explained that the moon was a liar. "See the shape of a crescent C? That stands for 'crescendo.' But the moon is a liar, so it is actually a 'diminuendo' moon. And when the moon has its round side on the right, it says 'diminuendo'—remember the Latin verb *diminuere*; but we know that the moon tells lies, so it's in 'crescendo' phase."

He was right. A waxing moon is always bigger than the moon the night before, until it reaches full moon. Then it becomes a waning moon and is smaller than it was the previous night until it becomes a new moon. As he had said, waxing moons always were curved on the right, like a capital D; waning moons were always curved on the left, resembling a C.

Back in my South African boarding school, we were looking

out one evening to the heavens where the Southern Cross dominates the hemisphere, not the North Star. I wanted to show off my expertise in astronomy by explaining that the moon was waxing, but my friend Philip contradicted me and asked how come the moon had been bigger the night before? I disputed this, but indeed the following night, the moon appeared even smaller. Oh the ignominy!

It turns out that the moon tells the truth in the southern hemisphere.

Learning to Appreciate Gourmet Cuisine

Food at boarding school in South Africa was only half as good as the food at school in Scotland. Porridge was served not once, but twice daily. We had corn meal or cream of wheat for breakfast and oatmeal for supper. The savagely boiled pumpkin gunge was particularly nauseating and many boys tried hard to avoid it. Pumpkin, a disk-shaped vegetable, had a white, hard skin and was a dark yellow inside. One fellow had pushed the yellow sludge under its white carcass and placed his knife and fork neatly together, signalling "all done with main course."

"Boy! Show me what is under your pumpkin skin!" bellowed the headmaster, at whose table he sat. Poor boy. He was forced to lift the pumpkin skin, and his non-compliance with school lunch rules was revealed. We felt for him—a prisoner led away for torture. We all looked down, not wanting to draw attention to ourselves, lest we also be chosen for the daily persecution of being forced to eat more pumpkin. He is a brave man, however, and he thrives today, having stared down congealed pumpkin.

The breakfast-cereal situation was worse in Africa. Porridge twice a day meant having to buy more food from the tuck shop. There was in fact nothing wrong with porridge. *I* was the problem—too fussy to eat it, so I regularly purchased my cereal. We boys wrote our names on the packages and could retrieve these extra victuals the following breakfast or supper. We did not understand contaminant containment, however, and sometimes we failed to seal up the cereal boxes. Occasionally, when the box was opened, a roach would scurry off, offended by the sudden light. The cereals were eaten anyway. We would rather share our provisions with local insects than stomach the porridge.

One last mealy note is worth mention. On speech day, breakfast was suddenly eggs and bacon and toast with jam. The eggs were delivered, not broken and swimming in a tepid pool of oil, but intact and sunny. We remarked that of all days, speech day was the least important to serve a decent breakfast because we would be supplied with edible lunch by parents later.

One schoolmaster, who understood, explained the reason breakfast was excellent on this one day.

"Boys whine that school food is atrocious. They always have done so. It is an honourable, traditional whine. But parents want to know that they are receiving fair value for fees. So when boys complain and parents ask what they had consumed for breakfast that very day, the boys have to admit that bacon and eggs, toast and jam were all supplied."

Rugby Teams: Who Wants Wullie?

From these anecdotes, the reader will not be surprised to find that I was not really happy in boarding school; it was not an environment that encouraged my growth. That's not to say it was thus for all boys, or even for me all the time. In historical perspective, I just think that it should have helped build my self-image, rather than deflate it.

Almost all my report cards from all schools alluded to my

characteristic handwriting. Some compared it to arbitrary arachnid ambulation across the page, with all eight legs well inked. An early but ominous report card from my South African boarding school contained the following remark as my report for science: "This boy is not brilliant." It was concentrated acid, and a blow to a young lad, especially one who thought himself more aligned to the sciences, since I obviously had no talent at all in creative arts. It was a severe strike to the self-esteem. Another report card slapped me with, "Rather slow to grasp ideas and not hard working."

If Wullie had little academic ability, he had even less ability on the sports field. At the various schools Wullie attended, when teams were chosen for cricket or rugby, he would wait anxiously to see if he would be the last selected. Sometimes the captains of these teams would find that the Wullie boy would be their eleventh, or fifteenth person by default, and more than once they said that they'd be better off without him completely. Maybe the opposing team could have him as a twelfth player. Then would ensue a competition between the two team captains, both defending their respective teams against having to endure Wullie on their side.

"Sir! It's not fair. We had to have him on our side last time," some friendly boys would object. One would hope that a school would challenge all its pupils to attain and exceed their best possible performance, but in fact those deemed of little athletic prowess were usually just ignored. At the age of thirteen and on, most of us have misgivings about our real personalities. In my case, the self-image was one of doubt and dejection.

Today, past middle age, I easily run four or five miles at a time and I'll warrant that, in our fifties, 70 percent of my peers from school cannot hold a candle to that.

Finding the Athlete Within

Believing back then that I was wholly hopeless, it came as a complete surprise to me in 1962 that I accomplished a 220-yard sprint in quite a respectable time—probably under 26 seconds. I began training, so as to lower that time. Later in the summer term I was to compete in the heats before the annual school games. In my heat, there was another young man, Paul, who was possibly the fastest man alive at the time. He could sprint 100 yards in about 9.1 seconds, and 100 metres in about 10.1. Had South Africa been allowed to send its finest to the Olympics, we felt Paul Nash would have taken at least a silver and possibly the gold medal.

On that hot sports day, Wullie took up his position and tried to look like an athlete. Kneeling down, with feet tightly sprung against starter blocks, he was in the next-to-outside lane on a semi-oval track, so that put him a little in front of his rivals, on account of the wider radius. Wullie looked behind him and saw his competitors pawing the ground, muscular men kitted out in the sleekest running gear.

Wullie didn't have the aggressive spiked running shoes favoured by these real athletes. In fact it hadn't occurred to Wullie to purchase running shoes at all. It was a cinder track and with no running shoes, his only option was to run barefoot.

Wullie knew to watch the starter gun and to leap forward upon seeing smoke from its barrel, instead of awaiting the "crack!" So when he saw the signal, he sprang forward. He thrust his feet ahead with every leap, hoping for an extra inch. Would Wullie have done better to take shorter strides? It certainly seemed that his legs couldn't actually move any faster, so any increased speed had to be achieved with longer strides. About 30 yards from the finish, Paul streaked past.

Wullie was doing well towards the finishing post and

The Hopeless Athlete

demanded an extra inch of stride from his legs, but his timing was thrown off and he fell full length onto the cinder track. He did scramble up, but with his forward momentum stumbled again right across the finish line, sliding in on his stomach and arms. Another competitor finished at that instant.

Did Wullie's centre of gravity cross the line before the other competitor or not? Would Wullie have been the second-fastest man in the world, had he finished in an upright position? It was of no consequence, because he was disqualified from the heat. The rules of track competition said that one had to finish by running, not by hurling oneself like a missile across the finish line.

While my self-image was not enhanced by this flailing display, I had to admit to myself that at least I had tried and that was worth something.

The Master of Physical Education

While I was still at private boarding school in Natal, I was to confront the charming Mr. F. He was ex–British Army and he liked you to know it. He was not a man for tolerating namby-pamby softness. No, he'd make men out of the mice, Wullie being one of those rodents. Mr. F. was the physical education instructor and if ever there was a sadistic P.E. teacher stereotype, he would be right up there with the paragon of role models.

First there was the sad episode when he wanted all the boys to do dead-man dives (dead-boy dives) off the three-metre diving board. I ascended the ladder cautiously and peered over. Three metres seems awfully high when one is actually up there.

"What's a matter wiv you? Are yeeoou chicken or sumfink?" yelled Mr. F. Just like the penalty for army desertion being worse than staying on the front line, I knew that there was no option but to go forward. The problem was how to make my body actually hurl itself off the plank, head first.

The head comprehended that it had to be done, but the body, which knew the head was actually quite a vulnerable part of the anatomy, was fighting with the head. The body said,

The Hopeless Athlete

"Head down the ladder, while you can." The head reasserted itself and demanded obedience from body. Body turned to go back along the plank before taking a running dive. This way, the committed mass moving in a particular direction would continue in that state unless acted upon by a force, at least according to the physics master.

There is an Oor Wullie story where he is scared to dive off the high board, and he is disgraced in front of his pals. He accidentally bumps a local bully who then chases him and inevitably he finds himself up the ladder of the high board. At that stage, there is only one course, which is to dive. From the cowardice of escaping the bully, Oor Wullie gains sufficient courage to face the high dive, after which he is redeemed in the eyes of his friends.

Alas, Mr. F., who by this time had mounted the ladder, was the bully. Thinking that the boy was about to become a chicken, he picked up my Wullie frame and launched it into space. No chicken, my wings did not spread and I fell—"gersplat"—onto the water almost ten feet below. Body suffered agonisingly from this belly flop and felt quite deflated. Pain or no pain, however, head managed to exact just a short moment of revenge against Mr. F.

My specific gravity exceeds 1.00, which means, as some friends have observed, that I am exceedingly dense. I just sank! The kerfuffle that ensued I could not hear, but when somebody appeared below the surface, presumably to rescue me, I found the strength, but more so the savvy, to slink away and surface on my own.

It was hardly the dramatic rescue from the film *An Officer and a Gentleman*, where the drill sergeant dives into the pool to assist a trapped pilot, but if Mr. F. had been caused even a few seconds of worry, it was worth the effort.

On another occasion, Wullie had been ordered to run, jump on a trampoline, launch himself high into the air, reach to the distant end of a gym horse and then land neatly upon his feet at the horse's far end. Several athletic boys accomplished this with grace. Unfortunately, Wullie jumped too low and crashed into the rear end of the horse. While colleagues were amused, Mr. F. was not. It was 6:30 a.m., midwinter, and a thick frost covered the playing field outside. South African winters are usually dry, but they can be colder than we imagine. The ground was frozen solid.

"Ta-eek orrff yor shews and yor socks!" commanded Mr. F. Wullie did as bidden, wondering how this might make him a better jumper.

"Raahnd a track, aahtsahd, na-eoo! At a dubboo. In yor bare feet!" And so Wullie put in a mile on a frozen track before breakfast while Mr. F. disappeared, presumably to the comforts of his eggs and bacon.

I recall only one other such delightful encounter with Mr. F. Wullie had been out on leave one Sunday, and being a fair-skinned Scot in sunny South Africa, he had acquired a sunburn, particularly across the shoulders. As luck would have it, in P.E. the following day, the boys were ordered to stand another boy on their shoulders. Posed just beside the wall bars for stability, they were to perform knee bends (squats).

"Excuse me, Sir," interjected Wullie, "but I have a bad sunburn on my shoulders, so to have someone stand in his shoes on them—"

"Oivah do wot I tell you, or you can be 'ad up on a charge of damaging army proptee, for that's wot yor sunburn is."

I Get My Stripes

Boarding school was obviously intended to be militaristic. South African private (fee-paying) schools were modelled on the British public school system and there were many similarities. The institution was intended to be tough, and

The Hopeless Athlete

South African society had become increasingly different from its European origins and civilising influences. Although the school remained admirably independent from the government and its policies, the ambience in the country was not healthy. White people did not always see or want to see how the basic rule of law was being eroded. Our teachers, including Mr. Gillespie (maths) and Mr. Pollack (history) were illuminating liberals when the lights of freedom were gradually being extinguished.

South Africa had endured a state of emergency and at that time, all school rifles had been confiscated. They were later returned, but their barrels had been filled with cement, so that these old single-shot, bolt-action relics were thus rendered even heavier. The boys drilled with these antique guns, and they drilled some more, because every year there was a competition among the houses. First-year boys were exempt from cadets, but in second year there I was, all dressed in khaki, boots polished to a mirror-like shine, with a cap resembling First World War German troop apparel; another ominous symbol.

It was not uncommon for cadets to faint in the sun, while endlessly standing to attention, rifle on shoulder. They were usually the fair-skinned ones, and after all, only mad dogs and Englishmen go out in the noonday sun. I was never English, so being out in the noonday sun must have made me an insane cur.

At times it was felt preferable to faint than endure. A soldier's myth circulated: by putting blotting paper in the boots, the cadet would faint. I didn't try it, not only because there was probably no evidence that the trick worked, but also there were penalties for trying it anyway, such as running around the parade ground with one's rifle held above the head for too many laps.

A commanding officer from a Natal regiment appeared at the school for our drill and deportment competition, and platoons were marched past. Wullie watched several other platoons go through their paces, moving as if all legs were connected by invisible rods, so well did they march in time. Then it was the turn of Wullie's platoon and they formed up. They marched out to the familiar "Left... Left... Left, Right, Left." Just before the dais where the brass peacocks were standing, the drill sergeant muttered under his breath: "Out of step! You on the outside towards the rear! Get it right! Now!" Wullie had been trained on how to get back into step, with a short half-hop, but this had been practised before the rifles had come back. His feet were back, but alas, the arms now were not. He was camel marching (left foot, left hand going forward at same time).

"Get it right. Stop camel marching," again whispered loudly under the drill sergeant's breath. Then came the next command, this time in full military scream, "Squad! Squad! Aaaaah eyeees right!" The drill sergeant was the only one meant to salute, but Wullie had got everything else wrong so, why not go off with a bang? He saluted—the only cadet in the squad to do so.

In the dormitory there was much talk about how this miserable man called Wullie had cost the house so many points. Natal Command was even heard to comment (apparently) on the incompetent cadet. I was the roast of the town.

The following year, our squad was drilled more thoroughly, later, for longer hours and on Saturdays. It came to the big day and Wullie's fellow soldiers teased him about not being out of step on the march past, and not to salute. Wullie was so worried about getting it right that when the squad sergeant screeched, "Eyeees right!" he knew he was meant to do something else with his hands than what he had done the previous year. The trouble was, his brain became a blank, so he saluted.

It was absolutely incomprehensible that a cadet could get this wrong twice, and Wullie endured many a sarcastic

The Hopeless Athlete

comment. So it came to pass in the third year that again they were to have a drill competition. Wullie had, by this time, figured out that concentration was key. One could not daydream on parade, no matter how hot the sun, nor boringly pointless the activity.

Wullie had even gained one stripe, which made him a lance corporal. As such, he now had to drill fellow cadets who had even fewer brain cells. He took this, however, as a great challenge and felt genuinely pleased that his small band halted when halt was commanded, and lefted when left was ordered. When the command was issued to "Maake as of jy loop, maar loop nie!" they did not start marking time until the command's last syllable (the command is translated exactly as "Make it look as if you are walking, but don't walk").

Too often, cadets heard the "Maake as" and immediately started stomping air, but not Wullie's troop. They awaited the final syllable, and only then did they mark time.

The day arrived. Wullie knew he had the concentration to keep his eyes where they should be, and his hands. He was polishing brass on his belt and wiping a speck of dust from his boots, when the drill sergeant appeared.

"Lance corporal!" bellowed the D.S.

"Sergeant!" responded Wullie in full soldierly fashion, even though his boots were still on the table in front and he had one hose on, and one set of toes bare on the floor.

"The march past today. Your leg has just been injured and you can't take part. Report to the duty nurse immediately. We can't risk a third mess-up."

Wullie was left to slink off to the sanatorium to tend the fictitious injury.

Are You Blind?

All white males, at age seventeen or eighteen, had to report for South African army call-up. It was a full conscription and medical fitness was assessed beforehand. A doctor was engaged by the army to assist in this process and in our final year, just before our exams, they came to our school. After some cursory chest listening, we came to the Ishihara colour-blindness test: a series of cards.

For those who have never seen them, each card has a bunch of different coloured dots, printed within a rectangle or circle. The colours are meant to be contrasting, and 92 percent of the world's males can see the number or pattern that is dotted in a different colour from the background. I belong to the other 8 percent, called anomalous trichromates. We don't see the pattern. What is a perfectly obvious dotty red "5" on a green background to most people, is just a bunch of lighter or darker, bigger or smaller blobs to us colour-blind misfits.

"What number do you see in that circle?" asked the doctor. It was a square, but I didn't think that was the question's objective.

"I don't see a number there, Doctor." The medicine man looked sharply, then flicked the page and tried again with another similar test.

"No number there either," I continued. The quack went ballistic.

"Now look here, young man. I am an important doctor. I don't have time for your games. Tell me what is those numbers."

I began to protest, but the man was almost frothing with anger. He was not going to hear anything I uttered. He tore strips off me for attempting to evade military service, proclaiming he was a doctor and too smart to fall for a trick like that. It dawned on me that the man had not the faintest idea what he was testing.

So I was destined for the army, colour blind or not. I sat my final-year exams, called matriculation, with a sense of foreboding, suspecting from my cadet experiences that military life would not be my ideal choice. As South African white society polarised into those pro-Government and those against it (and therefore traitors), I just knew that I did not belong in the pro-Government camp. Thank goodness I could fall back on my Scottish identity to preserve me, at least inwardly.

A telegram arrived at school one day, just after French exam: *"Annual intake too many for officers to train. Not required undergo military service this year. Deferred."*

This was one of the most fortunate events of my life. I had been reprieved. I thought that by the following year the situation might be the same, but perhaps with a compounding effect. They would have too many recruits from the current and the subsequent year.

I went on to take an unexpected first-class pass with distinction in maths. If only the telegram had arrived a few hours earlier, I might also have gained an excellent mark in French, with my newly elevated mood.

African Royal Wedding

Shortly before finishing school in 1964, Wullie had taken a trip to Swaziland to visit his sister. The trip itself was an adventure. Wullie alighted from the train in some South Eastern Transvaal town before dawn and waited on the dusty station platform. Later a bus ambled along and passengers, chickens, a lamb and a goat all piled on.

Swaziland is a small landlocked country between South Africa and Mozambique, and I stayed in Manzini ("Manzi" is Seswati for water). One day Wullie's sister and her husband took Wullie to a wedding. This wasn't just any wedding, it was

They Called Me Otherwise

King Sobhuza's, and it was a four-day experience, where the king could not himself be present all the time, due to matters of state. It was an event like other royal weddings, where the public are welcome to watch the proceedings, though Wullie obviously had no regal connections.

In an open field, along the road to the onomatopœically named Mbabane, the capital of Swaziland, the wedding party stopped at the venue (imagine the babbling sound of the Mbabane River). There were warriors who danced with *assegais* (spears) before them. They thumped the ground with their feet in a fearsome display, so that the earth trembled. At one stage, the bride's mother could be heard keening at the loss of her daughter to another household. The bride, in a lovely gesture, brought a blanket to wrap around her mother's shoulders, a traditional comfort.

The party carried on for several hours, in the heat of the open field. Later, a Swazi family invited Wullie back to their house for an ongoing celebration. Wullie walked over and as he arrived, a huge cauldron of beer was being passed around. Well, school rules forbade drinking any alcohol, even when not in school. The punishment for infraction was expulsion.

That wasn't the only dilemma. The beer was yellow in colour, with a curdled film on top, like thin custard. Wullie raised the urn to his mouth and was about to try and appear to drink, without actually drinking, when his brother-in-law suddenly arrived by his side. Wullie was whisked away. The beer never touched his lips. The brother-in-law had been to the same school years earlier and knew the protocol.

Wullie's disappointment at having the beer snatched away was short-lived. Imagine his utter amazement when he heard some lovely singing from a distance and looked over to see many, many young girls, about his age of sixteen, rhythmically dancing in a procession towards the ceremonies. From the waist down they wore tiny beaded skirts; from the waist up they were, every one of them, naked.

CHAPTER FIVE

Wullie Loses His Brains
Free at Last 1965 to 1969

"University is Not the Place for Him"

The nude girls marked the end of my innocence. I left school without a backward glance. But having finished high school and being spared from the army's clutches, I knew not what to do. Having no other thoughts, I enrolled in a bachelor of science degree program at the University of the Witwatersrand, majoring in mathematics and statistics. At the unsuspecting age of seventeen and three months I started my classes in maths, economics, psychology and philosophy. There were many distractions. Boarding school had been a monastic, cloistered existence. At university there were girls, shared classrooms and freedom from petty rules. At seventeen and with a matriculation behind me, I was wiser than I had ever been before, or have ever been since.

I went to parties, tried beer, wine and even rum, started dating and took part in many extramural activities offered by the university. I took judo lessons, went swimming, played squash, started weightlifting. I sang in the choir, reported for the student newspaper and worked on the student science council.

The last two were quite political and soon I found myself on daily protest marches against the government's Apartheid policies. The marches were quite dignified, because the faculty members often came too and we all wore academic robes in a long, colourful procession through Braamfontein in Johannesburg. There were speeches and demonstrations.

We distributed banned recordings of Martin Luther King's "I Have a Dream" speech. The student body invited Robert Kennedy to come to South Africa to tell us about how much better race relations were in the U.S. The South African government did not welcome this interloper, but they didn't actually deny him entry. Playing truant from my classes, I went to the airport as part of the entourage to meet him. Amazingly I was able to step right up to him and ask for an autograph, which he gave.

Looking back into the Jan Smuts Airport concourse, I saw Ethel Kennedy walking with absolutely no one beside her, so I approached and asked for her autograph too, which she kindly wrote. These prizes were thrown, as trophies, at the feet of my then girlfriend, Christine. She was Catholic, so anything from the Kennedys was special.

Unfortunately, I failed my major subjects at the year-end examination. On a resit I triumphed, and with a mere smattering of knowledge of the first-year course, entered second year. This was a year of complete abjection, for I had built my understanding of equations on a volatile foundation. There was a knockout punch after the dizzying blow of first year: I failed both mathematics and statistics. A letter was received from the dean, Dr. Balinsky, informing this miscreant student that under regulation R5, I could not be readmitted to the university. My cup was less than empty.

A friend's mother, herself a university lecturer, offered the advice that it was important not to make a habit of failing exams, because by one's failures one would be known. Surprisingly, this advice did not cheer my heart. How deep was the despair! The dean's office agreed that I could see him concerning the expulsion. My father asked to come along,

Wullie Loses His Brains

and in one way this was a supportive parental gesture, but perhaps I should have been made to wallow in my own muck without company. In truth, I was deeply ashamed of my academic failure and also doubted my future. This was not a proud following in my parents' and grandparents' footsteps. I was a disgrace.

Before the meeting with the dean, I walked past the university swimming pool and spotted a fellow maths student. She looked equally forlorn. I sat down and we began comparing our sins—chiefly, the lack of mathematical knowledge. She was to see the dean a little later. I remarked that I had seen a good job going as a shoeshine, to which Ada responded, "Wullie, you must be Jewish like me!" I admitted that I was not.

Ada replied, "You should be. You have a self-deprecating humour like a Jew. You'd make a good Jew! Whenever things go wrong for us—and can they ever go wrong, I tell you—we make jokes about it. What else can we do but make jokes? It helps get through the bad times."

It was a hot summer afternoon. I sat with Father, uncomfortably perched on wooden chairs outside the dean's office. After we were kept waiting a suitable length of time, we were shown in and again seated on upright wooden chairs.

"Dean Balinsky!" My father cleared his throat and commenced again. "Dean Balinsky, thank you for agreeing to see us this afternoon. I am myself a university graduate and know that my son has potential. He is a hardworking boy and I would ask—"

The dean waved his hand and cut my father off.

"Sir, if your son truly works hard and cannot pass either of his major courses, may I suggest that university is not the right place for him?" The softly spoken words were deafening thunder. This was complete humiliation.

Dean Balinsky allowed the gravity of his enlightening observation to settle into the skulls of the two men before him. The two rose to leave. Where mathematicians look for lowest common denominators, here had I become a lowest common demon. Perhaps I could get that job as a shoeshine boy.

Dean Balinsky had performed this act before and his dramatic timing was perfect. Addressing the younger and avoiding eye contact with the elder, he said, "We shall readmit you on a trial basis. If you ever fail another course, we shall retroactively invoke rule R5. Do I make myself clear?"

He had indeed.

Campus Years: Facing Apartheid

Although university was tough, South Africa was politically very active and an interesting country. Part of my academic failure had been due to taking part in those protest marches against the government, sometimes daily. We had some amazingly courageous and inspirational leaders. There was Margaret Marshall, later with the U.S. supreme court; Michael Stevenson, later president of Simon Fraser University. The Anglican chaplain, Father John Davies, was a steady beacon throughout those years. There were other fine leaders in South Africa, all examples to us, like Albert Luthuli, who won a Nobel Peace Prize in 1960.

Apartheid laws were widely repressive. To have sexual relationships across racial lines was illegal. We thought that if the religious right had managed to make their views stick, they would have banned all sex forever. So we were deliciously delighted when a Dutch Reformed Church minister was himself apprehended with his trousers down, in the company of a non-white girl. It only justified our best honed prejudices against the ruling clique. Father John admonished us for being uncharitable.

We protested, "It's the truth. He was caught, and

universities must always fight to preserve and expose the truth."

"You speak the truth in arsenic, rather than with humility; you should show compassion, particularly for the girl also," was his reply. He accompanied us on many anti-government rallies, as did our professors. This leadership from the university faculty was truly inspirational. It confirmed my belief in the Scottish liberal tradition.

Our sense of justice told us that Apartheid was wrong. Being committed to non-violence, I wondered what could I do to make South Africa a better place, even a tiny bit. It was important not to neglect my studies, but university is not just an exam hall. It should be an environment to help one grow in many dimensions. So although I studied very hard, I did not neglect completely the sociopolitical side of life.

A friend, Tony, had helped establish a school for black children near where he lived. It was not well financed like my school had been and supplying each necessary article was a struggle. Art classes? They certainly didn't have those because there was no paper or paint. A local newspaper donated a huge roll of blank newsprint and some paint brushes and paints, so I took these off to the school in Witkoppen, just outside Johannesburg, on Saturday afternoons.

With hindsight, my personal attempt to teach art really was an affront to those good black children, the teachers and their parents. If I wasn't very academic in the sciences, I had negative ability in art. Drawing even stick men is a struggle for my hand. Furthermore, my suggestions to paint animals or the seaside were met with blank stares. These children lived four hundred miles inland, had never seen the sea and did not encounter many animals beyond cows, dogs, horses and mosquitoes. They walked to my Saturday art classes anyway, some older children carrying their younger siblings on their backs.

At the end of those Saturday afternoons the children hung up their paintings with pride, washed the brushes and their desks, emptied the water from the cans, swept the floor, straightened the desks and then filed out. I went weekly and if it was a small attempt to break through the colour bar, it seemed appreciated by both sides. My art did not improve at all, but theirs did. Their first pictures were tiny, filling two or three square inches because they didn't want to waste paper. Later, they would fill a whole sheet.

Uncle Jimmy's Gourmet South Africa

You might think that life was grim for many people all the time in South Africa during those years, but family and fun go on and they helped people persevere, especially during the hardest times. Humour helped preserve our humanity, even in the humility of knowing that our protests might not be doing much good.

In 1967 Aunt Patricia, Uncle Jimmy and my cousin Gordon visited South Africa. Impish Wullie conspired with my uncle's great sense of humour to produce a South African delicacy for our visitors. Liz, my niece, was then a baby and so there was an ample supply of babies' bottles. We took some teats and covered them in white sauce. We warmed this up and then brought it triumphantly to the dinner table.

"Aunt Pat, this is a special South African treat. It's not actually in season right now, but we managed to get some from the butcher—'Octopus Nipples.' They're an appetiser for dinner tonight. You've got to try them."

Patricia eyed the terrifying mixture of blubbery stuff. "Oh, I couldn't. I couldn't. I'm sorry, I really am, but I just couldn't." Then she looked up for support from her husband and recognised that familiar, mischievous sparkle in his eye.

"Jimmy! Och, Jimmy, shame on you!" Aunt Pat collapsed into tears of laughter.

A Second Chance for the Bar of Gold

Partly in the hopes that a healthy body would make my brain work better, thus allowing me to pass exams, I had started weightlifting at university and eventually could press 70 pounds with one arm (only the right arm, mind you). Now why could I not have that golden opportunity again, down the mine as a child?

Visiting a trade show with my girlfriend, I spied a gold-smelting operation. What an ideal occasion to impress her with my strength. I asked the hot, harassed smelter if I could take the gold bar away, should I be able to lift it with one hand. The man hesitated, but sized up the slightly built college teenager. He took a risk. "You're on," he agreed.

Now I knew I could lift that amount, so I was about to be rich. A gold ingot is slightly conical in shape, narrower at the top than the bottom. My fingers gripped the sides. They sweated. They slipped easily up the side of the ingot, unable to achieve any purchase. Again I tried, but the cold gold just mocked my attempt. The demonstrator knew all along that he was safe.

I also lost the girlfriend, despite my prior gifts to her of the Kennedy autographs.

Save Every Golf Tee

Father had a great sense of the ridiculous, and he could make fun out of almost nothing, and just about everything. He could tease in that fashion where one is not quite sure if a joke is in play. There was the episode when he had been preparing a talk to the board of directors and had punched holes in a piece of celluloid, so that it might be filed in a binder. He picked up one of the small disks of celluloid that had fallen to the floor and, spying a pretty receptionist, went over to her, gently pulled down the lower lid of his eye and said, "Excuse me, but could you help me put my contact lens back in?"

Father was a keen golfer and thought that I should be one too. On one occasion, I was asked to make up a golf foursome with him and two businessmen. At the 10th hole, he used a broken golf tee and after he had driven off, he looked around for the tee. It was not to be found.

"Come along," encouraged the other golfers.

"I can't find my tee," lamented Father. The golfers beseeched him to ignore it, since it was broken to begin with. No, he just had to find it.

Finally he said, "Wullie, after the game is over, while we are at the clubhouse having a drink, you will come back to this hole and look for my tee." I soberly agreed to do so.

Incredulous, the two golfers turned on Father ferociously. "For goodness sake, it's only a broken golf tee. Here, we'll give you a spare."

Father would have none of it. "I won't have waste. Wullie has to learn the value of all things in life, and that he can't throw away a golf tee just because it's a wee bit broken. It's an essential part of learning to be thrifty."

Keeping the ball in play, I agreed, "Yes, Father."

Arrested for Carol Singing?

While at university, Wullie made a friend in Tony Brink, a geology professor and expert in mining engineering. He was a very liberal and honest man. He appeared to Wullie as someone completely trustworthy and Wullie respected the way Tony challenged the political status quo in positive, creative ways. Tony knew some people who had been arrested for treason, friends with whom he had on previous occasions shared Christmas Eve carolling.

Wullie Loses His Brains

At Christmas 1967, Tony invited Wullie and some associates out to go carol singing, and after serenading at some old-age homes, they found themselves outside the Pretoria Jail. Tony explained that these friends were inside and would appreciate the singing. An Afrikaner himself and, with this easier access to the then South African bureaucracy, he approached the duty jail keeper and asked if the troupe might sing to the prisoners. Permission was denied.

So the carollers sang from outside the walls, lustily intoning, "Bring us some figgy pudding, and we must have it out here." Lights went on in the prison: the singers knew the intended audience of their songs had heard. The jailer had too, and he stormed out, leapt into a khaki-coloured Volkswagen and drove off very fast.

Minutes later, he returned with a fully uniformed warden, carrying a swagger stick. He firmly warned Wullie, Tony and company that they were not welcome. They had disobeyed the jailer and as such he had the powers to arrest them. It being Christmas Eve, he would prefer if the carollers just scampered. Tony, Wullie and friends had made their point, and so they did not press on to defeat the South African Army....

On Christmas morning, we used to get a newspaper. There on the front page was a tiny reference: "Christmas carollers almost charged outside Pretoria Jail." My father looked up from his paper and queried, "You were Christmas carolling last night. Did you have a good time?"

Physics was Not My Subject

A few days later, Tony invited Wullie over for dinner. Wullie had been learning the mathematics of relativity theory in third year and there was another man present who asked what he was studying.

"Mathematics—we're on relativity maths right now. In

fact, I have found that the best explanation on the theory of relativity is written by Einstein himself," replied Wullie, puffing up his chest. The gentleman expressed interest and asked Wullie to elaborate. So, Wullie clarified as best he could, in lay terms.

The monologue continued for some time, with Wullie waxing on the issue of mass and how, when approaching the speed of light, it becomes harder to increase velocity because, according to the theory of relativity, the object's mass to be accelerated is magnified so much.

The gentleman looked perplexed. Perhaps Wullie had moved too quickly for him? He interrupted. "What about the possibility of there being masses already moving at velocities greater than the speed of light? Could they in theory exist? Perhaps they could move more slowly but never quite as slowly as light because a similar constraint would apply? They might have 'complex variable' masses."

Wullie was amazed at the depth of this question. It was an exciting idea, at once synthesising the mathematics of relativity and the branch of maths known as "complex variable." Could there be an entire universe coexistent with ours, but never accessible to us? The question alerted Wullie's antennae, and he paused to ask, "I'm a student, obviously, but what do you do?"

"Oh, I'm professor of nuclear physics at Witwatersrand University."

Final Reckoning with University

In third-year mathematics, the subject of topology caused much thrashing in my brain cells, and there were many points of inflection and undefined discontinuities within my cranial cavity. Towards the final exams, I studied later and later into the night. Mother always said she could divine my progress from the music that was being played on the record player. Melancholy music meant a mal mathematics mood.

At that time of political confrontation, some mathematics lecturers were deemed by the government to be subversive and they were subjected to house arrest, without trial or other recourse. Mathematics was corrupting the young men of Johannesburg. I went to the home of one banned lecturer and took private lessons from her. She was permitted to have one visitor in the house during daylight hours, so she tutored mathematics to earn a living. She was helpful and knowledgable. The government succeeded in making her a non-person, however. Today, sadly, I cannot recall her name, despite the success she had in dragging mathematics into my brain. . . .

There being a dearth of faculty within the department, an inquiry was made to see if a certain Professor Young were too old to teach. He could still stand up, so he was dusted off and brought in to teach real variable mathematics. In fact he was a brilliant man, and could stand at the front and write up entire proofs without looking at notes. He didn't even carry any notes, and sometimes would forget what he was teaching. However, he would ask the students and then take off from his last turning-off point.

One afternoon I went to ask a question about proofs concerning sines and cosines. "My boy!" muttered Young, with voice quavering, "My boy, if you can't understand that by now, you don't have a hope of passing, eh, of passing my final exam." I left Young's office, with Dean Balinsky's former warning reverberating in my head. I was scared, and it wasn't just about being an academic klutz. Failing my degree would diminish my opportunities and probably force me to stay in South Africa, at least longer than I wanted.

Like many universities expanding with the baby boomers, construction was ongoing, even during exam time. Noisy pneumatic drills were working nearby, but I failed to notice, being so absorbed in the questions. One problem required a lengthy proof that two expressions, A and B, were equal. This could be done by demonstrating that they were each equivalent to a third expression, C. With ten minutes to go, I had not tackled this question. By my good fortune, Dr. Carter, the invigilator, suddenly announced that due to the disruptive noise we had permission for an extra 20 minutes.

I set about proving that expression A equalled C, which took most of my remaining time. Proving that expression B also equalled C was more daunting. I started a new page in the book with the title appropriate to the proof and furiously scribbled many formulae involving B. I realised that I was going in circles while the clock ticked on linearly. Running out of ideas, I switched to expression C and proved once again that it equalled A. In desperation I wrote that since A equalled C (prior page) and since B equalled C (which I had not in fact proved at all), <u>A must equal B</u>. I underlined it.

"Stop writing! Put your pens down," boomed Dr. Carter. I somehow passed the exam and thereby achieved my science degree, having proved the obvious: A equalled C and therefore C equalled A. University degrees, however, not only test raw knowledge, but they also nurture the capacity to "hang in to the end," and we Scots have that tenacity.

The Real World?

Towards the end of the degree program in 1968, I had to consider career possibilities—what a nuisance! I was persuaded to sit an aptitude test with a major software company.

Some questions were strange. One concerned failure in light bulbs. If, on average, one in ten light bulbs fails and a man requires one hundred lit bulbs, how many should he purchase to be sure that he has sufficient for his hundred? There were five choices.

Well, I understood this stuff perfectly, because I had a degree in statistics, but my answer was not among the five possibilities presented. After the test was over, I approached the bench. "One of the questions is wrong," I offered. The young lady administering the test looked at this piteous creature who questioned the questions. It was like an inmate of an insane institution saying that it was the doctors who were all mad, and that he alone was sane. "The questions have been carefully validated," she huffed as she raised her nose in the air and stalked off.

The test results didn't come for several weeks, and then more weeks. Finally I phoned the computer company to ask about the outcome. My name was taken, records were searched and eventually an administrator came on the phone. "Your results indicate that computing systems is not a suitable job choice, so we didn't bother informing you of the result. Goodbye." Although I had passed my degree exams, my self-confidence was still low and this rejection did not enhance it. The stubborn Scottish nature asserted itself, however. I went on eventually to make a career in information processing, and gained international stature in computerised accounting systems. It was delicious spite.

Black Humour

Although the software company recruiters didn't want me anywhere near a computer, in fact I had to program the beasts anyway, during the seven-month work engagement I had in South Africa, following final exams.

I was employed at the University of the Witwatersrand as a statistician in the registrar's office. I had met a young black man, Jafta, on a couple of occasions through the Anglican chaplain, but any social encounter across racial lines was deliberately made almost impossible by the then government.

Places of entertainment, cinemas and restaurants were segregated by law. Still, we did try to force some congregation between white and black people. I use the word force, because inevitably, the get-togethers were a bit stilted.

Around lunch one day, I went into the computer centre. Jerry, the manager, was there, and so was Jafta with several of his colleagues. Jerry spoke up.

"This is Jafta."

Jafta glanced at me and looked away, so I interjected, "Of course. Jafta and I have met before, several times."

"Maybe. I don't recall," replied Jafta with a certain bite in his voice tone. "You know, all you whiteys look the same to us," he continued.

There was an instant tension in the air. Sparks are always dangerous around computers and Jerry looked suddenly uncomfortable. In Apartheid South Africa, that just wasn't the sort of comment that black people made to white people. On the other hand, some white folk often failed to notice black people properly and so did not learn their distinctive features, with the result that often you could hear them say that all black people looked alike.

I found Jafta's comment hilarious, and laughed. But the question was, did he? Suddenly a laugh broke from Jafta's mouth and his colleagues erupted in sympathetic guffaws. Sometimes a joke is only a joke if it's interpreted that way, and this was one of those occasions. Humour cuts across class and race. Jafta is a Scot, just as I am a Xhosa.

CHAPTER SIX

Scotland Regained
Saint Andrews 1969 to 1973

Leaving South Africa Yet Again

On a sunny day early in 1969, watched by my relieved parents, I graduated with a degree in maths and statistics from the University of the Witwatersrand. I had been fairly politically active, and this was not always a route to success in repressive South Africa. Scottish liberalism runs strongly in my family tradition, but it was difficult to practise that ethic. People who openly criticised the government could find themselves in trouble or even banned, as had happened to the maths lecturers, and to Ian Robertson, the head of the National Union of South African Students (NUSAS).

Since I did not have any investment in a career, and South Africa did not look like a good place for me to nurture my roots, I did what my family had done before: I moved. My next upheaval, at the age of twenty-one, was back to Scotland. My parents, while not exactly happy to see me depart South Africa, encouraged me because they knew it was the right thing.

I sailed for the U.K. in August 1969, and enrolled to take another degree at the University of Saint Andrews. I had obtained a South African passport when I was not required to undergo military training, and thought it best to emigrate before the authorities changed their minds.

Sailing from Africa to the U.K., I had ambiguous sentiments. I was leaving South Africa which I felt was home, but was also leaving because of political problems. South Africa was a warm climate, a land of plenty. I played squash weekly, or more often. I had finished my exams and succeeded, so there had been a calendar full of parties, among good friends. I did enjoy a glass of wine, even South African wine, and it was often a moral dilemma whether to drink the local product, or wine from some purer country, like France, that only detonated nuclear devices in the South Seas. Now I was to abandon that comfort zone, and 1969 was a year to redefine myself.

On the ship, a fellow passenger volunteered that I would have a hard time affording wine as a student. However, he could vouch that a certain Yugoslavian wine was competitively priced and was also similar to some South African white wines.

If I had guilt feelings about South African wine, I had equal misgivings about wine from a communist country. Were the commies not just the same as the fascists? However, I found that the price was right and, besides, several students seemed to enjoy this brand.

Imagine my shock many years later, when I discovered that the said Yugoslavian wine was indeed a South African product, just bottled and labelled in the communist enclave. So much for principles.

In South Africa, we were not supposed to be able to buy Swedish Electrolux products, but a subsidiary outside Sweden seemed to have no problem supplying goods. Parachutes were alleged to come from France, even if the French government was ethically totally opposed to the South African regime. Sanctions by many western countries just drove the commerce underground, or made it flourish in different ways. So much for trade embargoes.

The South African company Armscor became a sufficient supplier and then net exporter of armaments. In fact, the infamous Canadian Dr. Gerald Bull seems to have cut his teeth in arms production by perfecting a more accurate gun for the South African Army (see the movie *Doomsday Gun*, based on this episode).

A Lesson in Chutzpah

As a young man, I was still experimenting with what sort of person I wanted to be. Before going up to university in Scotland, I went to Geneva to visit a friend and of course took the opportunity to visit the United Nations, and also the World Council of Churches (WCC). The WCC was at that time active in denouncing the Apartheid regime and so it seemed natural that I would want to pay them a visit in Geneva. They proved much more "hefty lefty" than I had anticipated. There I met a radical man who seemed to delight in haranguing me merely for being a white South African, so not surprisingly I did not linger. . . .

The Palais des Nations was Wullie's next call, and with camera in tow, he found himself sent along sightseer corridors, on an ersatz sanitised tour. That was no good, so deciding to play his role differently, he returned to l'Hôtel des Eaux Vives, where he dressed in a dark suit, left the camera behind and bused back to the Palais des Nations.

This time, Wullie wandered the corridors at will. Custodians in uniform opened doors for him, but never asked who he was. He listened to speeches on hunger and food distribution, on water potability and on vaccinations. It was fun to see how far Wullie could push this. At lunchtime, he drifted around and found himself at the delegates' dining room.

The door was held open and Wullie went in. He was nervous about putting a foot wrong, and did not know if all meals were purchased by some sort of coupon system, available only to accredited diplomats. Wullie also realised that there would be many foreigners in the building, unsure of the protocols and the language. So, in his school-level French, he ordered lunch in this diplomats' sanctuary.

Alas, it seemed that something he said offended the staff member flicking crumbs off the tablecloth. Wullie was either too late, or they were out of the *plat du jour*. It wasn't the first or the last occasion in Wullie's life when his verbal fluency in French was not matched by his comprehension. So he sat for a while, unsure of what the restaurant staff member had said. It seemed that food was not coming his way, and eventually he left.

Probably Just A Coincidence

I flew back from Geneva to London and upon my arrival at Heathrow Airport, two of those freakish coincidences in life played out. I'm schooled in the logical positivist philosophy and thoroughly grounded in the empiricist tradition, exemplified by Scottish philosophers such as Adam Smith and Hume. It will be no surprise then that I do not believe in ghosts, phantoms, aliens from Mars nor in some unseen hand that patterns our lives. Coincidences are just that. They are governed by the same laws of probability that I had studied in my statistics classes at university.

Elizabeth had been a fellow student throughout all my maths and statistics classes at Wits. She was a lovely person in personality and looks, and occasionally on my lucky days she would give me a ride home in her small blue Mini. After graduation from Wits, in the late summer of 1969, we went our separate ways and lost touch. I worked for seven months in South Africa before leaving to attend my new university in Britain.

After touching down at Heathrow on that flight from Geneva, I was expecting to meet my close colleague Nicholas for lunch. I had also been pondering how I might find yet another friend, Mike, who was living in London. One could hardly try dialling all the eight million telephone numbers.

Off the plane, I boarded a red double-decker bus, the sort that trundles off to Victoria Station. Elizabeth, none other than herself, appeared out of the airport and deposited herself next to me. After a one-hour flight from Geneva it took three to get to Victoria Station, so there was plenty of time to catch up on old maths problems.

Later I went off to meet Nicholas, who was working for Lazard Brothers, the merchant bankers on Threadneedle Street. I was already a tad tardy by the time I reached the well-known street and I began walking in the wrong direction. Realising my error, but knowing that I might stray again, I thought to ask someone for directions. I tapped a random man on the shoulder, and the missing Mike turned around.

I still don't believe that coincidences are meant to happen. They just occur.

You Met Where?

Just before going up to Saint Andrews, I was invited to a party in London. My host said a few friends would be along. I travelled via the London underground, and as the train emptied, there remained just two passengers before the last stop. I eyed my pretty travelling companion. She had dark, short hair and her skirt was a mini, as they often were in 1969. Even from half a carriage away I could sense her perfume.

The woman saw me looking at her and averted her eyes, as did I. But then we both looked back and we could not suppress smiles at being mutually caught out. I wondered if we were destined for the same party and decided to be brave enough to ask. We were, and so we arrived together. The host greeted us warmly.

"Wullie, Sylvie. I see you already know each other. Splendid. Do come in—entrez."

"Yezz," chirps Sylvie, who was very shapely, and delightfully French, "We 'ave prevveeously met in ze tub." I reminded my host that we had only met in the tube.

Mr. Birrell's Grocery: Ye'll Have Anotherr Glass?

Saint Andrews is a university with several hundred years of tradition. In 1969 students still wore scarlet academic gowns, which were not only colourful, but could be wrapped around the body as partial defence against the cold North Sea air.

It is also a custom that senior students look after the new arrivals, who are called "bejants" or "bejantines." They help them find their way around the city, show them where their classes are, which bookstores to avoid and when to wear full academic gowns to dinner. Sometimes a senior man might introduce the bejantine to more important aspects of life, like skipping classes so they might pursue other activities together.

By and large, the tradition is honourable, useful and much to be encouraged. Historically the new students presented their senior men or women with a pound of raisins (*uvarum siccarum*) as a thank you for this service. Raisins would have been highly prized in prior years as a food rich in iron, besides being pleasant tasting. More recently it had become traditional to present something else derived from grapes, namely a bottle of wine.

When I arrived at Saint Andrews in 1969, my home country was a pariah on the international scene. The South African government's racist policies were unacceptable to the purer folk of other western countries, and equally unacceptable to many whose practices were much worse. It was no longer possible to purchase South African wine or sherry in Britain:

this gesture was thought certain to bring about the South African government's swift capitulation, which it did—within twenty years.

I was in a dilemma. How could I despise all things South African, especially wine, when I was partly of that society myself? Our doctor's wife back in South Africa, a grande Parisienne dame, used to utter dreadful comments about all "*choses Sud-Africaines.*"

"But I myself am South African, Madame," I would protest.

"Pffft, you are not. If ze cat chooses to 'ave 'er keettens in ze oven, zey are not cookies," she would pronounce with finality.

Despite some misgivings, I decided to attempt to purchase a bottle of South African wine, in Scotland, for my senior man. With conspiracy in mind, I furtively set out to a grocery that might sell such a bottle.

"Good afternoon. I'd like to buy a bottle of wine—a South African bottle, if you have any." The lady fixed her steely gaze on me. Had I asked for something unmentionable, by mistake? Perhaps I should mutter apologies and dash out from the store, hoping never to be recognised again.

"You'd better speak with Mr. Birrell himself."

The genial Mr. Birrell appeared, so now I was committed and could not run for the door.

"What can I do for you, Sir?" he asked gently. This was worse than a young man's first visit to the birth-control section in a pharmacy.

"Do you have any South African wine?" I asked *sotto voce*. It was like asking if they had rainbow-coloured assorted packs of condoms with devil's faces on them. Was this young man really that perverted to be requesting South African wine?

"Aaah, it's no' verrah popular the noo. Ye'll underrstand. There hasn'ae been much demand for it in a wee while. You'd better come to the shop storeroom."

They Called Me Otherwise

That was it. I was to be detained, probably imprisoned in a tea chest until the suitable authorities could be summoned to deal with this miscreant student. Would I be sent down? Deported? What would my family think of such a besmirching, particularly after all they had done for me? Could I cut a deal with Birrell right now, maybe even claim to be from a radical-left student organisation, just checking up to make sure he didn't stock any?

I walked slowly, as a prisoner to the gallows, into the grocery store's dim interior. A lone yellow light under a broad enamel green shade bravely threw a few weak photons of light to cheer the room. There were boxes of tomatoes, crates of wine. As my eyes adjusted to the light I saw seemingly endless jars of jam all stacked up. Sacks of sugar and flour and cases of whisky were piled neatly, high into the corners.

I savoured the seeming normality as long as I could, but I knew that the magic would be broken. I would be condemned for my insolent request. The shapeless bundles against the wall would become my fellow condemned companions, *les oubliettes* of 1969. (Les oubliettes means "the forgotten ones," and refers to prisoners of the French Revolution left to rot while incarcerated in La Bastille or worse prisons).

"Ah think ah have a few bottles at the back," Birrell volunteered. He disappeared for a moment and came back triumphantly with three dusty bottles of wine. "Ah've had these since forrty-six, just after the warr. Nobody wanted to buy them. Of course, they may not be any guid. We'd better open one."

I was drawn to the back of the grocery and ushered into a chair, which had probably been handsome in her youth. Now she lacked a back, and stood unsteadily on four unequal legs.

Mr. Birrell produced a pair of wine glasses out of thin air, pulled up the chair and a pair of tea chests and proceeded to open one of the bottles, whereupon we sipped the marvellous red liquid, aged for twenty-three years. "It's no' tha' bad. Ye'll have anotherr glass?"

Scotland Regained: Saint Andrews

We chatted about many issues, not just South African wine. Meat was differently cut in Scotland than in South Africa. The Scots ate more cured ham and Mr. Birrell was a fund of information about the country and the traditions in

Saint Andrews itself. He was of a generation before mine, so obviously knew all about the hardships of wartime rationing. He was also familiar with some South African brands of tinned peaches, though they were also unobtainable at that time.

After a wee while, Mr. Birrell again offered a glass. We sat in the back of his store and quietly drank the whole bottle between us. After that, he gave me a discount on the remaining two bottles. I thought I should repair to Saint Salvator's quad, where I was meant to attend a lecture on metaphysics.

I lurched into my class, but I remember nothing of the lecture on the nature of being (ontology) from Mr. Bryant.

Years later, when buying liquor in the province of Ontario from the Liquor Control Board store, I again felt like a criminal as I approached the counter with my slip filled out, requesting a bottle of South African wine. In 1973, the board sold liquor from a series of warehouses of clinical appearance, although they have changed much since. The contrast between the Scottish hospitality of Mr. Birrell and the Ontario LCB could not have been more marked.

Eros At Madame Tussauds

At the completion of the first term at Saint Andrews, I went to Aunt Nan's in Glasgow for Christmas and Hogmanay. Thereafter I bused down to London to visit Pat, a fellow student who, it turned out, had also invited her boyfriend to stay. Luckily she was a hostess able to rise to the occasion and we were all made to feel welcome. She suggested we meet Melanie for lunch.

"Melanie?" I inquired.

"You know, the Canadian girl," responded Pat. There were not many Canadians among the 2,000 students at Saint Andrews. Although I lived in the same residence as Melanie, I didn't think that we had actually been introduced.

I had a morning appointment at the Bank of Scotland on the Haymarket, where a former colleague of my father worked. Where could we meet afterwards for lunch? I thought I could find the centre island at Piccadilly Circus, next to the statue of Eros. Well, what better spot than Eros can you suggest for meeting a couple of girls when you are a young man? It was Melanie's twenty-first birthday and we decided to go to lunch at an Indian restaurant. Melanie paid for lunch and I bought a bottle of wine. It was a most happy day.

A couple of days later, I was back on the bus to Scotland for my second term. At that time, I sported a moustache and on the first evening back in university residence, I met Melanie and a group of friends in the hall. Someone asked to borrow coffee, so I nipped nimbly up to my room to obtain the required item. Upon passing the mirror, thinking that the moustache looked scruffy, I quickly shaved it off and hastened downstairs again. The coffee powder was accepted, but not a soul noticed my changed appearance. I had obviously made quite an impression!

A couple of weeks later, I went skiing with a few friends. The skiing was not excellent at Devil's Elbow, being very icy, so I limped home with a few bruises. Melanie appeared and helped salve the wounds. Melanie is the daughter of an eminent professor of zoology at the University of British Columbia in Vancouver; he was at that time on his second sabbatical in Oxford, and she was on exchange for a year at Saint Andrews. On his previous U.K. sabbatical, in 1958, he had also taken his daughter to Madame Tussauds in London, just after Christmas. This time, I romanced the girl from Canada with spring daffodils and dinner at The Grange. It took us just a few months before we were engaged to be married.

Politically Correct Language

In the summer of 1970, I had permission from the British Government to earn a bit of money by working as a laboratory assistant. I was an alien South African and so was obliged to request a work permit. With a Scottish father, I could have applied successfully to become a British subject. That seemed too easy, and also a bit mercenary, because it would have substantially reduced my tuition fees. I also knew that I intended to emigrate to Canada once Melanie and I had married.

With my training in statistics, I was particularly useful to research psychologists requiring a data analyst and my tasks during those summer months included endless statistical calculations. After two months I wanted a break, so I travelled to Canada to see the family of my fiancée Melanie, back home from their sabbatical. Sitting down to dinner one night beside some distinguished guests, among them university professors, I realised my good fortune. Here was a cultured family, in a free country unlike the renegade South Africa. What more could a fellow wish than to marry the girl of his dreams, from such a family, and live in a free country?

The talk turned to gardening. My future father-in-law knew much about plants and medicines, about art and history. Then he mentioned his goldfish pond. The goldfish had become somewhat depleted again.

"The coons keep taking them," he opined with distaste. I gulped, feeling shock and dismay rise in my gorge. How could a professor, of all people, accuse coons of taking his goldfish? First of all, there was absolutely no proof. Second, why would blacks want them? Thirdly, how could he with any conscience use a term like "coons" to refer to non-white people? Cultured, distinguished people indeed! It was almost enough to call off the engagement. However, I needed to marry a girl from an English-speaking country other than South Africa, and Melanie seemed prepared to have me. (This marriage for citizenship has lasted only a third of a century so far.)

Years later, living in Vancouver myself, I encounter coons periodically. They are bold creatures, with white faces against a black background. They are furry and slightly larger than domestic cats. In fact, raccoons are becoming far too comfortable with city living in the Kitsilano area, but coon is not a racist term for non-white people.

First Home: Westburn Wynd

After my brief exposure to Canada, Melanie and I returned to Scotland in September 1970. She had originally been an exchange student, but Saint Andrews is a small university and when she applied to finish off her degree there, the university authorities knew it had something to do with being engaged to another student—me.

Towards the end of the academic year in June 1971, we had to find a suitable home in Saint Andrews. The wedding was to be in September back in Canada, so we needed somewhere to live by then or earlier. Married student accommodation didn't exist as such in those days. A friendly solicitor in Saint Andrews, for whose children we babysat, was instrumental in assisting us to rent a charming house in the city centre, near the library. The house owner insisted on meeting us first, so I dressed up in my new Galloway tartan kilt and set off to the pub for our appointed meeting. Mr. McT. had suggested the Cross Keys, which wasn't the most elegant pub in town, although the hotel was pleasant.

A silence came over the workingman's place of refreshment as I stood on the threshold before entering the pub, wearing my new duffs. The Galloway dress tartan is nothing if not loud. It is bright red and blue, with a stripy touch of green too. You cannot not see it. The Galloway tartan forces itself through your eyelids like a thousand-watt halogen interrogation lamp. There I was, fully kilted out in my black Argyll jacket with its silver buttons, my three-tasselled sealskin sporran, its polished silver surround and my sgian dhu (that small black dagger kept in the sock top).

The pub had a plain floor and a decidedly smoky atmosphere. Nobody was unkind enough to suggest that I was out of place and we sat down to nurse half pints, waiting for the owner of the house to show up, which he didn't. After a while, we wondered if there wasn't another bar up in the hotel. There was, and McT. was in it, and about to leave since his prospective tenant had not shown up. The regulars in the pub rolled their eyeballs as we left, but nobody said a word, at least until we were out of earshot. The kilt passed muster with Mr. McT., and the house was ours for two years.

Westburn Wynd was the loveliest first home a student could ever have desired. It was central to the town and it had a secluded garden. Melanie went back to Canada to perfect the wedding preparations. I moved in and set about cleaning the house. The home had been inhabited by students for a while, but its history was long and impressive. Over 200 years old even then, it had at least five fireplaces and such charm that it had obviously been the home of a prominent city landowner. The sitting-room windows looked out onto both the lane and the back garden, called a "lang rig." This back garden had an eight-foot-high stone wall around it, and the west side collected the morning and daytime sun, so that in time it burst forth with a fragrant family of sweet peas, in a tangled residence against that warm wall.

After long habitation by single students, some dirt on the stairs looked original from 200 years past. The solicitor's wife was insistent that I must spruce up the home before I could bring a new wife into it, and immediately marshalled resources and organisation to make it more habitable. A new yellow kitchen floor was laid. Michael and his wife arrived to help paint. She was days away from having their second baby, but perhaps nest-building was strongly directing her, because she painted most of the living room.

A window pane had become broken but I knew I could easily fix it. The frame was measured twice before I walked over to Wilson the glazier. The glass was cut, and I returned home with the pane, which had cost only £1.50. It was exactly the frame size and thus just a fraction too big. However, as luck would have it, I had earlier purchased a glass cutter, also £1.50, so I slid the implement about 3 millimetres in from the pane edge, scoring it reasonably evenly. I tapped it gently, then took pliers to remove the surplus. The entire pane broke into several pieces.

On the second trip to the glazier, I ensured that the glass was slightly smaller than the frame and again handed over my £1.50. This time it fit perfectly, so I kneaded some putty in my hands and put a spot in each frame corner to hold the glass in place. When I bent down to retrieve more putty, the pane pained me on the head, breaking cleanly into three pieces.

The third trip to the glazier in an hour brought the retort, "It would have been cheaper to have me come and do the job in the furrst place. You'll get a discount for quantity this time: I'll only charge you fifty pence."

Third time lucky.

Sunday Post to the Rescue

Despite my Scottish ancestry, I was considered an alien at Saint Andrew's University, not only on account of my strange looks (remember my big ears and the knuckles that trail on the ground), but because I was a South African citizen at the time. Aliens were not meant to work for pay while in Britain, because they usurp jobs. They also had to renew their student residence permits with the

They Called Me Otherwise

government annually. Woe betide the student who became too politically radical!

I was to be married on September 9th of 1971, in Vancouver, Canada, and had managed to find an excellent price on the return airfare, a mere 56 pounds sterling. In about July, well before the wedding, I sent off my passport to some government office in London for a visa stamp, accompanied by the appropriate forms in quadruplicate. I wanted to ensure that the British government would permit this alien to re-enter the U.K. after our wedding. After a few weeks, I wondered what had happened, so sent a second letter, following up. Post in Britain, then as now, is usually delivered within a couple of days at the most, so by the end of that week, I became a bit worried.

I went to the General Post Office and purchased a registered letter form with prepaid reply. Not only was this guaranteed to be delivered, but a reply was also guaranteed because the postman waited for it. Alas, such rules presumably applied only to private enterprise, because the government ignored its own post office rules and no reply was returned.

At this stage I really was getting concerned, being due to leave for Canada in a few weeks. Not arriving at the church on time because of a mere missing passport would be a lame story, so I decided to phone the office. After several attempts to get a phone that actually rang, I found I was indeed speaking to the office. They would have to put me through to another department. To the second petty bureaucrat I explained my tale.

"Ah, that would be alien students. Hold on."

The next line rang, and rang, and rang, then went "burr" and finally went dead.

I tried another prepaid registered letter, with the same lack of result as the first. I was desperate, what could I do? I appealed to my old chum Oor Wullie in the *Sunday Post* newspaper. Well, to be more accurate, I wrote a letter to the

Scotland Regained: Saint Andrews

Sunday Post. The newspaper published a customer complaints section each week, with stories of electric blankets going on fire, toasters that didn't toast and car warranties not honoured. I typed them a letter, outlining that I wanted my passport back, so that I could fly to Canada for my own wedding. How could a government be so callous as to keep a man and his sweetheart apart?

Bill and Melanie's wedding day, Cecil Green, UBC, 1971

They Called Me Otherwise

Late one evening, as I returned to the David Russell Halls of Residence from sailing with my friend Michael, a reporter from the *Sunday Post* awaited me. He wanted to know the story of this Scots boy, a South African just by accident, who desired nothing more than permission to attend his own wedding, and was suffering so much anguish at the hands of that government down in England.

I retold my sad tale as I shuffled through my mail. There, in a "Her Majesty's" envelope, was the passport. It was duly stamped, but there was no word of apology or explanation. The *Sunday Post* had certainly been instrumental in getting my passport back, but did I really want the story published, now that the issue was resolved? The reporter was understanding and, true to his word, never did publish the *Post*'s success over petty plenipotentiaries. Oor Wullie had rescued me again in an hour of great need.

Cowardice, Courage and the Comic John Cleese

Some people thrive on bureaucracy. Others strive just as much in attempting to tear it down and challenge the status quo.

Students elect the rector at Saint Andrews. This is a very democratic practice, ensuring that the students are represented at the highest level in the institution. At different times, they have elected characters probably not deemed serious by the university establishment, such as a cricketer and a radio announcer. They also elected J. M. Barrie, author of *Peter Pan*, who gave a famous rectoral address, "On Courage," exhorting the students toward this lofty virtue. From 1922 to 1925, Rudyard Kipling was rector.

In my time we elected John Cleese, the star of Monty Python's Flying Circus. He gave a marvellously satirical address entitled "On Cowardice," the perfect counterpoint to his predecessor's speech. One evening as I was serving dinner at Andrew Melville Hall residence, who should come along for dinner but Mr. Cleese himself? I served him a dollop of potato to accompany the haggis we had for dinner.

"Is This Yoor Spo'lump?"

My car was a Morris 1100, a vehicle with great propensity to revert to iron oxide. These rust buckets were common in the U.K. Their front-wheel-drive design and hydro-pneumatic suspension were innovative indeed—it was just that production quality did not match engineering ingenuity.

Having retrieved my passport from Civil Service (sic) clutches in September 1971, I flew to Canada to be married. The car needed repairs as usual, so it was left at a local garage. When my bride, Melanie, and I returned to Scotland after our wedding and retrieved the car three weeks later, the garage owner said that a wee side window had become broken, but he had repaired it at no charge since the car was in his care.

A week later, when driving on a dark road after dinner, I leaned over to switch on the spotlamp which was mounted on the front bumper. The darkness was as impenetrable as the tripe we had attempted to eat in boarding school, and I did not seem able to see any better with the spotlamp turned on.

A couple of days later, I noticed that the fire extinguisher was not in its usual place. Then I thought I had probably taken it into the house before going to Canada, and had forgotten to put it back. In those days, I always carried a fire extinguisher in the car, having seen a vehicle burst into flames in Johannesburg some years earlier. That driver was obviously accustomed to such behaviour. He promptly produced an extinguisher, smothered the flames and nonchalantly hopped back in the car and proceeded.

At dinner one night with several guests, there was a peremptory knocking at Westburn Wynd's door. No additional guests were expected, but outside stood half the Saint Andrews police force, namely one policeman.

"Uz thus yoor spo'lump, Surr?" he asked.

It was indeed my spotlamp from my car. I instantly had visions of incarceration, perhaps even torture in the Tower of London, for I knew exactly what had happened. The highway code stipulated that such lamps must be mounted not less than 18 inches from the ground. I had measured, and found my spotlamp to be half an inch lower, but I had not corrected the installation. The law's long arm had finally caught me.

"Well, I know it was mounted too low, but I'll have it put right immediately. Really, I promise."

"Thus uz yurr stolen spo'lump, Surr."

"My spotlamp wasn't stolen."

"Aye, when yurr carr wuz a' thuh garridge."

"No," I replied, a bit confused.

"Oh, did he no' tell ya aboot that? Yurr carr wuz stolen a wee while back from the garridge doon the road. Anyway, the thieves took your spo'lump but they brought the carr back. We caught them on anither car theft and asked if they wanted to confess to any ither crimes, and they said they'd taken this Morris 1100 but had returned it because it was so bad, there was no point in getting caught with it."

First Christmas Married

It was the custom, from the days my mother had asked Eric the shipping magnate to stay for a meal, to invite people who were alone at Christmastime to become part of our family, and Melanie grew up with similarly generous traditions. Her father and mother entertained countless graduate students over the years. So when we came to celebrate our

Scotland Regained: Saint Andrews

first Christmas together, we thought to invite fellows in Saint Andrews who were similarly far from home.

First there was Gertrude from Germany, whose speech had a guttural gait. Then there was Abe, an abbot from South Africa, studying at Cambridge, and lastly there was Ira from Los Angeles. He was actually living with us over the whole Christmas period, since university residences were closed.

We were friendly with the Presbyterian chaplain, and shortly before Christmas he called to advise that there was a package awaiting us at the butcher, and this proved to be a turkey. Melanie baked Christmas cake and mince pies, bought a tree and purchased small gifts for her new husband plus three foreign guests.

Mid morning on December 24 there was a ring at the door, and there sat Gertrude astride her bicycle.

"Christmas! I want to spend it by myself. Ziss is unique opportunity to spend Christmas by myself, zo I will try it. Thank you. Goodbye."

I looked down, a trifle dejected, and noticed that the morning post had just come in. There was a letter from Cambridge, and guest Abe said he just could not afford to get up to Scotland at that time.

At lunch, Ira, who was Jewish, mentioned that he had no wish to spoil the religious holiday and that his hosts should be free to celebrate it as Christians, according to their own traditions. Now there was nothing exclusive about the intended lunch, but sadly, Ira felt that this was a religious meal, rather than a fellow-student repast.

Wullie, his new wife, and a turkey? The kind Presbyterian chaplain was out of town, but the Anglican chaplain was home, so we invited ourselves there for dinner.

Sometimes one absorbs extra guests at Christmas, and sometimes one is the absorbee. The spirit of giving and sharing is what is really important.

Wine Connections: Starting a Tradition

To start our new home in Saint Andrews, my father had kindly sent a small crate of wine. This could have been demolished in short order with help from friends, but I realised that it was my chance to begin accumulating a "cellar." And so a rule was born, that if one wanted to consume a bottle, one had to replace it with two. Could not afford to buy two bottles of wine? Then we could not afford to drink one. Over time we built up a cache of about 50 bottles, purchased mainly from Mr. Birrell.

After graduation from Saint Andrews in 1973, we were making plans to emigrate to Canada, me following in my great-grandfather's footsteps, and Melanie returning home.

We realised that we could not easily take the wine. What a delicious dilemma! The only solution was to consume it, and so the last months in Scotland were a series of merry dinner parties. (Yes, some bottles might have been commie wine.) Close friends Matthew and Sue helped us reduce the cellar size, and nearly did us the honour of delivering their first child in our house.

Sometimes the friends one makes in university remain close for the rest of life. We have been fortunate in this way. The wine-drinking tradition we established with our good friends has been maintained through three decades and across continents. We have celebrated friendship many times between the 1970s and the present, and been thankful for being able to make merry together, comparing notes on children and reminiscing about the good old student days. We know we are always welcome among these Scottish friends. They and their friends bailed us out of tight spots later in life.

CHAPTER SEVEN

Return to the Land My Great-grandfather Farmed

Graduate School in Canada

Wullie had applied to do graduate studies in Canada, and was accepted by Queen's University in Kingston, Ontario. Canada was home for Melanie and it was also where my namesake grandfather had been born in 1875. So it was with anticipation of more university life that Wullie and Melanie flew to Canada in August 1973. During the next few years, with the assistance of some superb teachers, Wullie regained his brains. Accordingly, his self-confidence grew.

All new students in graduate school were required to sit four examinations after admission. While one student passed them all, Wullie passed three but didn't quite get through psychopathology at first sitting.

Dr. Friedman called Wullie in and proceeded with an impromptu *viva voce* exam.

"What can you tell me about left-hemisphere brain damage and co-ordination? Can you outline any connection between occipital-lobe traumas and motor skills? What do you know of Dr. Luria's studies on war wounds affecting frontal lobe and the ability to plan? Specifically, are you familiar with any studies concerning left temporal-lobe brain trauma and handwriting or other small motor skills?"

Wullie answered the barrage of questions as best he could, but the last one on handwriting and temporal-lobe lesions did not ring any gongs in his cranium.

"Have you yourself ever suffered damage, such as a severe kick to the left side of your head? If not, can you explain why your handwriting is so indecipherable?"

Wullie had again not passed psychopathology.

The reasons were not altogether poor handwriting. Wullie had suggested that some antecedents of mental illness, perhaps even causes of mental disease, were biochemical. Another faculty member explained that Wullie had to explore how mental illness was a learned, or conditioned phenomenon.

"But in many cases, I don't believe it is," Wullie protested.

His teacher persisted.

"If you want to pass the exam, you had better acknowledge the role of conditioning in the development of psychopathology. There is a famous experiment where Pavlov conditioned dogs to respond one way in the presence of circles, and another when there were oval shapes. He progressively made the ovals closer and closer to circles. The dogs' behaviour became increasingly neurotic, which shows that inappropriate conditioning can be a precursor to mental illness."

"Not always," argued Wullie.

"Just make sure you can quote the experiment," retorted the faculty member.

Wullie obtained permission to sit his exam in a private room, where he typed his answers about dogs. He passed the exam and, to this day, wonders what biochemical events surrounded Pavlov's insanity.

A Home for One's Children

The student apartment complex at Queen's did not permit babies or children. So with a wean (wee one) on the way, we had to find other digs. We hatched a harebrained scheme to buy a house on a student income, and a real estate agent took us to see some lovely homes at low prices like $45,000. But he quickly lost any interest upon discovering that even this sum was way beyond our pocket.

Another agent, more sympathetic, showed us some houses at $38,000. "This house is still beyond my means," I remarked and then the real estate agent asked exactly how much did I make. Five thousand dollars was the scholarship, and this sum was muttered at the agent. At first he was enthusiastic, until I mentioned:

"Five thousand is my annual income, not monthly." The poor agent had just wasted his time on a complete loser.

Wanting to retrieve something, he added, "There is this place on Victoria Street, which I and another agent own, but I'm not sure you'd want to see it."

Well, we did see it, including the storm windows hanging from rusted hinges at odd angles at the rear, the rotted playhouse in the back garden and the bits of furniture, including an old washing machine, turfed out onto the lawn (sic).

The house was purchased for $24,000 and became a home only because it could be subdivided into two suites. Rental income would help with the mortgage.

The existing tenant was instructed to leave, which she reluctantly did. Melanie's brother David helped to renovate, on several occasions, and without his expert assistance we certainly would not have had a livable house.

One weekend we were outside sawing wood and a small boy walked by, hand-in-hand with his mother.

"Are they fixing that place up real good, Ma?" he questioned.

I winced at the grammatical mistake, and then again at the mother's failure to correct it. She replied in the affirmative.

"Ma, are they no good too?" junior inquired. It seemed that the house had a reputation.

However, it became home for four years and saw two children into the world. Fiona was born the day the South Vietnamese Government surrendered to the Vietcong, in April 1975. Alex was to follow fifteen months later.

The house came with some accoutrements. There was a piano bench and a couple of chests of drawers, each with mirror. One was delivered to Paul, a fellow graduate student, on the roof rack of our small Datsun. Upon detecting large families of woodworms, he kept it for under ten minutes.

The double bed was also interesting. When turned upside down, we saw what looked like a black bottle brush wedged between the coils. The bottle brush turned out to have a pair of eyes. It was a mummified squirrel.

Sex Ed. in Jail

Grad school at Queen's was also a culture shock, a bit like Wullie's experience of boarding school at ten. Wullie continued to drift through life without seeming to interact with it, but the university environment wanted him to participate, to form alliances, to take sides.

Wullie and Melanie arranged a party for the graduate students. Their contribution was a turkey, already basted and ready for demolition. When they arrived at the grad house with the turkey held aloft, the party was already in high gear. Wullie remarked that someone had thoughtfully brought incense to enhance the ambience. There were some knowing winks and nudges from fellow students. Not one to climb out of a hole, but rather more inclined to keep digging deeper, Wullie remarked again about the incense.

Return to the Land My Great-grandfather Farmed

"Do you really not know what that is?" queried Harriet.

"Incense!" Wullie affirmed. Anyone could tell that sweet smoky smell was incense.

"Nooooo!" responded Harriet. "Think again, you oaf!"

Wullie thought, and decided not to be caught in Mary Jane's clutches, so left the party immediately. For all he knew, perhaps his fellow students proceeded to make a hemp stuffing, once the turkey was beyond his care.

Now some may say that this departure was evasion, but it was to have beneficial consequences.

A year later, besides being in grad school, Wullie began teaching computer systems at the community college. It had something to do with two children, a wife and the need to eat. Wullie didn't actually know much about business computer systems, but had written a few programs for scientific research and needed the income. He had to learn quickly, and Wullie did.

The college could not offer a full teaching load in business computer systems, so Wullie was asked if he would also like to teach developmental psychology to the incarcerates of Collins Bay Penitentiary.

Luckily—because he could not have taught without full clearance—Wullie passed the RCMP background investigation: no outstanding possession of weedy substances on his record! In fact, Wullie's job was to teach life skills in the jail, and this included biology and development. So it happened that a high point in Wullie's career was teaching sex education to the inmates of a fairly high security prison. That early comprehension at age eleven, of model-ship stands fitting together in eternal embrace, finally paid off.

The teaching situation was unique. Where else does one have to teach after passing through five electronically controlled gates, arranged such that the second does not open until the first is completely closed? There were bars around the high windows of the classroom, which looked out onto a barren exercise courtyard.

The prison staff did not venture much into Wullie's arena of learning. The teacher was somewhat left to his or her own resources, in the company of about a dozen inmates. Wullie took charts of female anatomy into the prison and tried to explain to the inmates how it all worked technically. For some reason, this brought only howls of laughter and derision. They had difficulty taking this section of the course seriously.

One prisoner stands out in memory. I'll call him Mr. Y. In the course of the course, Wullie made the heinous mistake of asking what dastardly deed had brought the prisoner there. Wullie was only trying to make conversation and show an interest, but it seems that he had broken a key rule.

A sudden silence, black as pitch, filled the room. One prisoner left. Another one looked at his feet, and a third examined a speck of dust on his hand. Mr. Y. picked at one of his teeth, while looking down. Suddenly he looked up and drilled Wullie's body with his piercing dark eyes.

"I was a contractor," answered Y.

"So what did you actually do? Fiddle the books?" asked the naïve Wullie.

With disdain, Y replied, "I don't think you fully understand the meaning of 'contractor.'"

I slowly realised that my life's work was not destined to be with the prison system, and determined to finish up my doctoral degree at Queen's as soon as possible. Besides, someone higher up in the seniority scale of the community college's union decided to return unexpectedly from maternity leave. A cascading effect caused me eventually to be bumped out of a job.

Putting My Best into a Ph.D.

As graduate students, we were permitted to enroll in courses unrelated to our direct studies, and I elected to take accounting in addition to my doctoral load. Professor Lawrence in the school of business agreed that I could take the course, and then as an aside asked, "Do you know anything about computers?" Did I ever. So I began teaching Commerce 324 in the School of Business at Queen's. The college door had been closed, and another much more enticing university portal had just opened.

The students at Queen's business school were dynamic and challenging. Queen's is always jostling for a top spot among Canadian universities, so these young men and women were among the very best. They often challenged what I lectured. In some ways, to lecture a course like this made me feel like I was an imposter, an actor being a university professor, rather than the real thing. I learned, however, that it was less important to be knowledgable than to encourage the students and act as a facilitator, assisting us all to discover new frontiers. Inevitably their questions made me think too, and taught me more. I didn't always know the answers to their questions, but teaching in that stimulating environment was some of the most fun I have ever had. . . .

Getting down to research, I chose to study sleep and the effects of alcohol consumption on it. One might imagine that this is an extensively researched topic. Queen's University boasts an internationally prestigious sleep laboratory and I was privileged to work there with two fellow Scots, Dr. Alistair MacLean and Mr. James Cairns, and Dr. John Knowles from England. I look back on that time in life as being exceptionally fulfilling.

My particular experiments focused on differences between effects of laboratory alcohol and the stuff people actually drink, such as bourbon. This is not a trivial difference, because in fact the extra chemicals in bourbon, which are not present in lab alcohol, can be quite toxic. They are collectively known as "congener substances."

Without incorporating a thesis in this book, we found

They Called Me Otherwise

more variability in the way sleep patterns are disturbed by real booze than by lab alcohol. Of course, some of the congener substances are also present in red wine. The "red wine effect" is quite well known. Some people unfortunately suffer headaches after drinking even moderate quantities of wine, more so red wine, and it may be that the additional substances like tannins, higher alcohols and sulphites are one of the causes. With practice, fortunately, I seem to have grown out of the red wine effect.

Dr. MacLean also taught me much about statistics, putting to good use what I had studied in such depth earlier in life. Most of all, the exceptionally high standards in the laboratory made me more meticulous about detail and subsequent analysis of results. In that lab I was bathed in the best of Scottish empiricist tradition, matched with an analytical/deductive philosophy. In the preface to the thesis, I say that my supervisors and advisors extracted from me my very best, then demanded and achieved even more.

CHAPTER EIGHT

In Business in Vancouver

Play-acting for a Living

Our family moved west to Vancouver in 1978. The doctoral degree was not quite complete, but well on its way. Once the decision was made, we thought, "If it were done when 'tis done, then 'twere well it were done quickly." It was essentially a decision to leave the dream-like university life and adopt the new persona of a harder-headed businessman. To this day, I'm not sure I ever knew what I wanted to do when I grew up, but in those years I played several new roles.

My primary reasons for switching career included a lack of jobs in experimental psychology. Those available were usually postdoctoral fellowships: interesting, but hardly stable for a family of four. Having taught some computer courses both at college and at Queen's, that area seemed the most likely source of a job.

My "almost Ph.D." proved to be quite the handicap when applying for positions in computer systems departments. I was advised to drop it from the résumé and somehow fudge those years in Ontario. I did this, was granted an interview, received a job offer and started working. Only then did I fess up to being about to defend a doctoral thesis.

Melanie and I flew back to Queen's for graduation in October 1979, and my proud parents came all the way from South Africa to witness my transformation. Roland Michener

They Called Me Otherwise

was the chancellor, and Senator Eugene Forsey, recipient of an honorary Doctorate of Law, gave the convocation address. Forsey was of course a strong federalist and did not have much use for the constant whining among the provinces. He mused that increasing provincial power would be followed by a change of Canada's coat of arms to ten jackasses, all feeding off the same tree.

On that particular day, I wore a royal blue tie with Canadian maple leaves on it. Forsey looked at my tie as I came forward to be capped with my Ph.D. in psychology, and leaning forward he said to me:

"A worthy tie: Keep the asses at bay."

That was over a quarter century ago. So did I use psychology in my job? Never! And always! I'm still working in the trenches of computer information systems, but along the way realised that many graduates in computer sciences could run circles around my paltry knowledge.

The solution was to take an additional qualification, this time as a professional accountant. It didn't make me a hotshot book fiddler, but it did allow me to pretend to the computer folk that I had some accounting knowledge to offer, and claim to the accountants that I could help navigate the arcane world of computers. My play-acting worked, and I am living proof that you can fool some of the people all of the time, just not the same people.

Bu$ine$$ Lunch

With a broad education and wanting to be categorised neither as computer programmer nor bean counter, I sometimes assume a character that is above my actual station in life. It can get Wullie into trouble when the act is sufficiently convincing.

Having actually gained employment in forest-products

In Business in Vancouver

companies, Wullie's career seemed established. So he was sent to a computer systems conference as one of the speakers and met a charming gentleman over dinner. He remarked that should Wullie find himself in his home city, please to give him a call and perhaps they could have lunch.

The unexpected event happened about six months later, and Wullie found himself invited to lunch at an expensive establishment. After a fine meal, thanks were offered, expressions of return of hospitality were exchanged and Wullie set off for South Africa, which was the main destination in his travels at that time.

As luck would have it, Wullie found himself six months later in the same city yet again, en route to another conference, so he called the insurance company where the man worked and asked if he might reciprocate lunch. The invitation was gladly accepted. The gentleman, Mr. Russell, thought it would be appropriate to invite a colleague who worked more closely with software than he did, and Wullie agreed that sounded like a grand idea. Mr. Russell suggested that since Wullie didn't know the city, perhaps he, Russell, could choose the venue.

The group met in the company foyer and repaired to the restaurant, where they were greeted by men in full-length morning tails. They knew and were anticipating Mr. Russell's party. The waiters slithered silently towards their reserved table, where the guests were seated amidst flurries of starched napkins whisked onto their laps. Menus appeared and Wullie inwardly gasped in horror at items like wine at $37 per bottle—that was the least expensive. Main courses were $30 at least. Mr. Russell also asked if they might have a bottle of mineral water. It arrived quickly and another $12 racked itself up on Wullie's mental till. Vegetables cost another $11 per serving, over and above the main course.

Towards lunch's end, Wullie discreetly went off to the washroom. The waiters, hovering obsequiously, had assumed a French air. However, on overhearing them in the kitchen, Wullie discovered they were obviously not French.

The bill eventually arrived. It was about $220 for lunch for three. This was more than Wullie's monthly mortgage payment in 1988. Wullie gulped and produced his credit card. Wives and children were never treated to such meals—how could he justify a lunch like this, with this man almost a stranger?

The story has a happy ending. Wullie continued on to a software convention in Monterey, giving another address, and there he met the director of sales for the Walker software company that was sponsoring the convention. Wullie recounted the story, at his own expense, so to speak.

The salesman guffawed. "What did you expect when you took out the insurance company's finance director?"

Unknown to Wullie, the gentle Mr. Russell was none other than finance director of a very large corporation. How was Mr. Russell to know that this Wullie was peon number 1143 at his institution, just a Glasgow commoner (keelie in local parlance) and not at a similar level to himself?

The kindly salesman said that since the episode had resulted from a meeting at a prior conference, it could be legitimately considered a client entertainment expense, couldn't it? "Tell me the amount."

"Two hundred and twenty dollars," Wullie offered, voice lowered.

"My, but we did eat well, didn't we? Say no more, it shall be paid."

Success and More Success

For my parents' golden wedding celebration in 1988, I went back to South Africa and, while in the country, thought to look up the S. A. Breweries company, which used the same financial software as we did, Walker Interactive. It turned out that my father had originally taken their general manager on board at his chartered accountants' firm, Alex Aiken & Carter, so I had a natural introduction.

I was whisked away from the Braamfontein offices to a location somewhere towards the airport, in a chauffeured car. At the firm's computer centre, after introductions, we chatted around their table about different computer system implementations; eventually the topic steered itself around to the data-query package, used for management reporting. The staff at S. A. Breweries had a useful, pithy article on how to understand this obstinate piece of software, and they would be pleased to find it and share it.

A tattered article soon appeared, and as soon as I saw it, I mused, "I know the author quite well."

The executives looked at me and then down at the commentary. I had written it myself and shared it the previous year at an international conference. Here were my own words being thrown back at me. I was famous. They were surprised and, I hoped, reasonably impressed. More was to come. We talked on about some intractable problem and they asked how we had managed to conquer that particular restriction. We didn't, I explained patiently. IBM had told us, as had the software vendor, Walker, that this limit was inherent and not just changed by a simple configuration.

"Oh, but we do have a solution," explained Lydia. "We thought that they just told us that. We're accustomed to South Africans being excluded from all sorts of commerce, on account of the Apartheid situation. We knew there had to be a way and assumed they wouldn't tell us because we are pariahs. So we solved it ourselves, but wondered if you had the same solution from IBM and Walker."

I was able to take this solution home to our boys. I led them on, saying that S. A. Breweries thought there could be an answer to this problem, but our gurus shook their heads and said it couldn't be done—inherent restriction in the software, you know.

"They have actually solved it!" I exclaimed, and with that impetus and a little discussion, we had the same solution implemented within a couple of hours. South Africa had then, and has now, some international-class expertise.

South Africa–to–Vancouver makes for a long pair of flights and, as usual on my way home after this trip, I stopped off in Britain to stay a short while with my good friends. Over a glass of red wine, Sue, a headmistress, was telling me about one of her class topics, ecological damage to the Pacific West Coast rainforest. As someone whose livelihood is earned in the forest-products industry, I have to admit to a certain sensitivity on the subject. So I decided to get some Canadian information for her to share with her classes. Canada House on Trafalgar Square was my obvious source and I marched off there, full of intention.

Inside, I explained to the receptionist, "I want some information on West Coast reforestation practices. A headmistress here in the U.K., friend of mine, is discussing ecology with her classes and I thought you might have some pamphlets on the subject. Another topic concerns forest fires and how they contribute to dioxins, and—"

"Nothing like that," she cut me off. "Perhaps you should try Seaboard next door. Do you know who they are?"

Seaboard is a consortium that handles export lumber from Canada. It's owned and managed in proportion to the amount of business each exporting company puts its way. My company is the major player in Canada, so I replied:

"Of course I know Seaboard, we own them." By this time she was already not paying any attention to me at all, but was talking quickly and in a hushed tone on her phone. The boyfriend was obviously much more interesting than my mundane request. Seaboard was literally a few steps next door and I went up in the lift to their offices. As the door opened, a man was standing right there in front of me, slightly stooped forward, wringing his hands like Uriah Heep. I moved to the right, attempting to step beyond him, but he looked at me straight and bemoaned, "We had no idea you were coming. I'm most terribly, terribly sorry. We should have had a car at Heathrow for you. Uhm, ahr, please do come in. This is most unexpected and I really am awfully sorry."

I was completely mystified at the effusive and flattering greeting. He must have mistaken me for somebody else. I pressed the rewind button in my brain, reviewing the past two minutes, and suddenly all was clear to me. This was quite delicious. I could not resist the opportunity to assume a different persona, if only for a moment.

"The general manager is actually away at meetings all day. Oh dear, what shall we do? He will be most upset to know that you arrived and he wasn't here to welcome you. In the meantime, what can I do for you, er, Mr., er, Mr.?" The poor man didn't know my name, and why should he? It seemed that the less I said the better, for a while.

"Price of lumber holding well on this side of the pond?" I interrogated him. "What is today's random-length price?"

"Let me see, it seems to be holding at about a hundred and ten. That's pounds sterling of course."

"Of course," I agreed.

"I'll assemble the staff to meet you as soon as I can round them up," he added. "While I do that, can I get you a cup of tea?"

I thought that would be splendid, but then he persisted:

"I have to confess, Sir, I'm most awfully sorry, but I still don't know your name, and if the staff are all going to meet you . . ." he trailed off. I realised the charade could not continue too much longer. Just before he disappeared to have someone boil up the kettle, I admitted that I did not own Seaboard. I was merely pawn number 1143 in one of the consortia companies that did. He was so relieved, and couldn't be angry. No harm had been done. I did get the cup of tea, though he didn't have any pamphlets on forestry practices.

Family Threads are Rewoven

I don't believe in coincidences, except as governed by the normal laws of probability. Things are not "meant to happen that way." Nevertheless, one Saturday afternoon in 1990, I went down Burrard Street in Vancouver to a store called Computer Station. The site is now a cinema complex, or a car dealership. On that day, I wanted to purchase diskettes for my computer. I presented my MasterCard. The sales representative looked at my name and remarked, "We have a Galloway working here too. He's over there."

I took one look at the young man and knew he had to be the grandson of my father's brother David. David had gone to America; my father had gone to Africa. The families had kept in touch only loosely and I had never met most of the American Galloways. The startled young man was embraced in a bear hug, and I said, "You have to be David Galloway's grandson. I'm sort of your cousin."

Some connections in life are priceless; for everything else, like diskettes, there's MasterCard.

If I can define one characteristic as typically mine, it's that family comes first. We stick together, we pull together. So this meeting was exceptionally serendipitous. The African Galloways and the American Galloways were reunited, almost forty years after I had last seen David's grandfather, my Uncle David. He had come to Africa and brought me a Hopalong Cassidy cowboy outfit.

To rediscover family and find they share a common decency, even the same sense of humour, is to realise a treasure chest of riches. Not only that, it turned out that David and I share a keen interest in software solutions.

Film Stars Invade My Gym

In my quiet life thus far, I had almost met Prince Charles, actually stood momentarily next to some Kennedys and served potato to John Cleese. They wouldn't remember me, but these luminaries provide some colour to us keelies....

When one is young, one can punish one's body, but years of working at desks, first studying to obtain degrees and qualifications and then working to earn a living, makes the body change shape. I had to start using the gym.

After a game of squash one day, my friend Doug Sinclair and I returned to the changing room only to be barred entry.

"They're filming *MacGyver* in there. I'm sorry, but you can't go in."

The rescue attempts of the TV hero MacGyver were much more melodramatic than my tortoise rescue from the swimming pool. Alas, I never came close to perching high on a stranded cable car, helping passengers escape some treacherous situation as he had done, but here I was in the same fitness facility.

Indeed, the hero was in the Men's and I was in a hurry.

"I have a meeting in 15 minutes. Must have a shower right now." An exquisitely made up young actress, with large brown eyes and auburn hair cascading in ringlets over her shoulders, stood by watching.

Someone with a clipboard and a headset mumbled, "Sorry. Tell you what, we'll get you a room in a local hotel where you can have a shower."

"Meeting in 13 minutes!"

"Sorry. Nothing else we can offer."

"Why can't I just use the change room. I don't care if there are camera people around or not. Doesn't worry me," I offered magnanimously.

"No, that would not be suitable at all," retorted the film crew, looking aghast.

They Called Me Otherwise

Dreams of being in a movie faded.

"Tell you what, you could use the Women's change room," one of them countered. I brightened considerably at this suggestion. It was like being invited into a forbidden club, an holy of holies. Keeping me at bay, a club official (a young woman) marched into the change room and barked:

"There's a man coming in to use the change room in one minute!"

And so I entered the sanctuary and looked around. There didn't seem to be a single soul present. I showered, lathered well and lingered, but eventually, with no sights nor sounds of any ladies, I dried, dressed and departed—none the wiser about women's locker rooms.

Were there people in that change room at the time? If so, they were just extremely well camouflaged. For my inconvenience, I was given a bottle of B.C. white wine, but not the opportunity to share it with the gorgeous brown-eyed film starlet who had been hovering around the set.

Like the Prince of Wales, MacGyver had also just failed to meet me in person.

The Sheecret of Shuksessh

As I gained confidence in computer systems expertise, I was sent across to the U.K. in 1992 to present a talk at a computer users' conference. The British organise these particularly well and we enjoyed a marvellous banquet dinner towards the meeting's end, with excellent French red wines, easily obtained due to Common Market membership.

Mikey, an astute man gifted with a sociable and customer-centric personality, and I talked shop late into the evening. We had met at several conferences in North America and the U.K. The topic turned to the data-exchange module for loading information between computers—we couldn't get that to work in our company at all.

"In some terminal emulators," voiced Mikey, "there's a field on the screen and it should be visible and unprotected. In some versions, that seems to be turned off. Just change it and your data exchange will work."

It was 11:00 p.m. in the U.K., so just midafternoon back in Vancouver. I found a British phone, deposited loads of coins, pressed button A and eventually my colleague Bareld answered.

I began foggily: "Turn the protected non-visible field on the screen to Visible Unprotect on your terminal emulator and the data-exchange module will work." It took a few tries before Bareld understood who was calling, from where and about what, but he did as bidden, and Mikey stood next to me as the problem was solved in Vancouver. That alone made the return trip to London worthwhile, because we had 1500 of these bits of software installed in our company, and we had just opened a new dimension in its use.

Sipping another glass together at evening's end around midnight, Mikey and I put the world to rights, and shortly before retiring he decided he would let me in on a confidence. "You know, Wullie, the key to the secret of success, with this software . . . Mark my words! . . . The key to success is . . . the cross-reference file."

I repeated: "The key to the sheecret of shucksess, I mean suckshesh, is the crosh . . . 'ference file." . . .

Back in Vancouver, I settled in to work, and our computer system purred along very well. Except one afternoon somebody pressed an Enter key and the entire system for the whole company congealed and went into slow motion. It was taking screens five minutes to respond, instead of the usual sub-half-second optimum suggested by IBM as best for human productivity. The system eventually came back, but we didn't know why the slowdown had occurred.

"You have to fix this urgently," my boss, Dave, insisted. "This is absolutely awful. Do something about this before you work on anything else." He might have said that I had to invent a cure for senility. I had no idea where to start, so I whinged,

"Dave, this could be network, or database. It could be that coincidentally several users—"

"This is your assignment," he cut me off. "Fix it. If it happened before, it will happen again." Then he softened just a bit. "Many of our user community have great faith in your ability to pull these kinds of rabbits out of your hat. I'm sure you'll figure out the problem."

That was it. I was sunk. I really didn't have an iota of an idea of where to begin. What Oracle would wisely guide me, if only I could consult it?

"The key to the sheecret of shucksessh is the cross-reference file." Infuriatingly this gratuitous information jumped into my brain. The more I wanted to think about possible reasons for the computer slowdown, the more the phrase taunted my thoughts. It became like a tune in your head that won't go away.

So I looked up this cross-reference file. Found it. Opened up its contents. It was full of junk information dating back years. It was like a log of all sorts of now-useless information, like what products had been sold by what salesmen in 1986 from what department. It was designed to speed up access, but nobody had thought to purge from it the now-irrelevant bits of information.

We figured out how to do that, shaved 20 percent off the size of our entire database and immediately the system became more responsive. We didn't suffer any of those awful frozen screens either. Wullie had saved the day, with a strong dose of Mikey's help. I was a hero. The solution was so obvious, and yet so easily overlooked. I was sent off to another international conference to expound on this newly discovered efficiency—with due credit given to Mikey (Michael Lane).

"Call Hotel Security!"

Success with computer systems does not depend only, or even largely, on technology. Sometimes it comes down to being able to play the right role in the right way at the right time. My new project was organising a company internal conference on how to use Walker financial computer software to best advantage. Optimistic estimates put the attendee count at about 30.

I had been fortunate to attend several international conferences. My boss permitted me to go as long as I gave a presentation, since that lowered the attendance fee. Then he decided I should always present two talks, thereby earning double discount, one for me and one for him. It was sensible to take back some of our conference knowledge to our fellow employees who had to use the software.

Perhaps I'm a natural choice to arrange a conference, because I can improvise on my feet and pick up quickly on cue—or miscue. As this event drew nearer, more and more employees indicated their intention of attending. Coast Inn of the North, located in Prince George in central British Columbia, was asked to provide a meeting room for after-hours socialising and, since it was the time of hockey playoffs, my colleague Carl insisted there be a television available.

For non-Canadian readers, it has to be understood that ice hockey is the national religion here. Teams across North America compete for the Stanley Cup, playing the best of seven games in an elimination series. By the time of our conference, Vancouver had won two and lost three to Colorado.

On the evening of the sixth game, after the conference events, we all gathered in the hotel hospitality suite and the TV was turned on. It produced intermittent hisses and much jagged fuzz on screen but nothing else. This did not bode well and there was already tension crackling like an electric charge in the suite. I contacted the hotel front desk and they immediately arrived to rectify the situation. The game had started already, so the clock was ticking.

The hotel employee asked for our tape to insert into the VCR.

"We don't have a tape. We want to watch the hockey."

"Ah, we assumed that this was a business meeting and that you had a tape to view."

"We don't. We just want to see the hockey."

"The VCR works fine, sir."

"We don't want to look at an old hockey game. We want tonight's."

"No problem, sir. I'll just plug it in to the cable outlet."

Five minutes went by while the luckless employee searched behind sofas, couches, tables and the fridge for the cable outlet.

"I'm sorry, sir, b-but there isn't a cable outlet," he stammered. At this stage, Carl announced menacingly that if we didn't have hockey within three minutes, he would lead a breakaway party, leaving for a local bar.

I went back to the front desk. I needed that cable.

"We're sorry, sir, but there isn't cable in that room. We can't help on this issue. Perhaps we could send up a few more bottles." I gingerly tiptoed back to the hospitality suite, with great trepidation.

"That's it. We're leaving," announced Carl. He turned to me with a sneer: "How could you be so absolutely incompetent as to not check into the TV?" Some people already were on the phones, checking the score.

I knew that my entire conference hung in balance. For a moment I despaired, but then I bolted back down to the front desk.

"Umm, about the cable."

"We're very apologetic, sir, but as we have said, we can't do anything about it." Attention was diverted to a new guest registering at the hotel.

"Ahem! Would you call hotel security!" I barked, in my most authoritative manner.

"What?"

"Hotel security. Call them immediately."

"Sir, we have already said that unfortunately, we cannot supply cable TV in that room. Hotel security has nothing to do with this issue."

"My life is in peril! I need a bodyguard with me when I announce we can't have hockey. I must have protection!"

The concierge cracked up laughing and ordered a bell man up to the room immediately. Soon, by dangling from windows a few stories up, he and an associate were able to throw cable from window to window, from room down to room. They plugged in the cable. The TV blinked to life, and we watched as Vancouver evened the score to one-all in the first period. My conference was saved.

"Just Who Are You Guys, Anyway?"

Maybe employees in the computer systems department are propellerheads some of the time, but they can also play at other roles, perhaps seemingly clandestine ones. In 1996 a group of employees, including Wullie, flew from Vancouver down to San Francisco for a meeting with the software company; they were trying to establish the software company's future direction, and see if it coincided with their own intended computer architecture. When several people are all travelling to exactly the same destination for the same reason, it is economical to fly them down on the corporate plane, rather than pay for six airfares return.

The company's twin-jet Cessna Citation already had several MIPs (more important persons) to drop off in Boise, Idaho, where the company had a manufacturing operation, so the passenger manifest portrayed nine people, plus pilots.

Wullie scanned the lounge in the executive-jet terminal, becoming more alarmed as each second passed. Everyone looked more senior, and this did not bode well for the seating arrangements. Wullie would probably get what is affectionately known as the "jump seat." It is the toilet at the plane's rear. Fortunately, it has a regular seat covering so one does not have to spend the flight "in the can," so to speak. And so it came to pass.

Wullie sat with shoulders and head bent forward for the two-hour flight, because the aircraft topology has a rear wall that slopes in towards the ceiling. The other jump-seat disadvantage is its isolation. Being located between the two rear-mounted engines, it is also noisy. So nobody speaks to the jump-seat passenger. Fortunately two MIPs alighted in Boise, so the other passengers allowed Wullie out of the lavatory for the remaining flight hop.

San Francisco was brilliantly sunny and the pilots made a perfect touchdown. One always compliments the company pilots on their perfect take-offs and landings. (In truth, they are skilled and always conduct superb landings.) A white stretch limousine rolled onto the tarmac after the U.S. Customs official had asked, "Where y'all frum?" Again, it made sense to hire one vehicle for the ride to Marathon Plaza downtown, rather than make six passengers take buses.

The meeting went well, so that by midafternoon, Wullie and company were free to fly home. They had all worn dark suits, since the meeting had demanded some formality and appearance of power on all sides. They played the parts of powerful men, and going out into the sun, all donned dark glasses. The limo driver (a new one) asked what they did. "Forest-products company, Canada," grunted somebody. Somewhere out near the United Airlines terminal, the six men in black realised that the exact location of our plane was in doubt. It had made a short sortie to another location between

In Business in Vancouver

dropping us off and the collection hour. The executive-jet terminal had to be somewhere nearby.

After patrolling up and down in the area for 15 minutes, Roy dialled someone on his cell phone and eventually was patched through from Canada back to the pilots, who were only a quarter mile away. The limo driver was instructed where to go, and he proceeded until he came to a sign that stated "Department of National Defense. Authorized persons only." He was getting angry, because he had been led astray, but Roy ordered him to continue. He protested, but Roy is tall and carries an air of authority.

The quarter mile further on there was a barbed-wire fence, and tall, though open, gates. A sign read: "Department of National Defense. Entry strictly prohibited except to those on official Defense business. Report back to the gatehouse. Do not proceed beyond this point unless in possession of an official DND pass." There was no local gatehouse and again the hapless driver was instructed to proceed. He probably began wondering if he would ever see his family again.

At that point, the jet came into view, with the pilots standing attentively outside. They always do roll out a red carpet and they had this time too. Everyone scrambled out of the limo and headed towards the twin-jet Citation.

"So, just who are you guys, really?" questioned the chauffeur.

"Don't ask, and you never drove us here today," deadpanned Roy through his clenched teeth.

Three Strikes: Dining Out in Prince George

Now that we knew more about the software direction, my boss decided we needed to offer some training to company personnel. The team was to be sent north to cold Prince George. I knew I had to be grateful. The company might have given me time off, banished me to the Bahamas and put me up in a five-star hotel, but my perk was more special than that. I was to work up in Prince George for a whole week. We were a team of five. The first day we presented a series of seminars on the software package.

At the end of the afternoon, we tidied up the conference room and stowed away some equipment, so it was 6:00 p.m. when we arrived at a local steakhouse, hungry and thirsty. It turned out that my class were there also, and we five joined them. However, no sooner had we arrived than they rose from the table and departed. Had my course presentation been that bad?

Our meals arrived; my steak was deposited at my place. The waiter trod on my foot, so the foot was hastily withdrawn with a cry of protest from me. The waiter's reaction was unusual.

"Oh! Your foot, sir! Did the earth move for you also, when we touched?"

He was trying to be either funny or rude, I wasn't sure which, but his behaviour was completely inappropriate. I shrank and attempted to pull my injured tarsals towards myself, but the waiter interpreted this as me getting up from the table, perhaps to confront him. Fisticuffs next? The waiter fled, muttering that a customer was after him.

If that wasn't strange enough, when the bill arrived, it was huge, more than double what we expected. We couldn't possibly have had twelve main courses among five of us.

"The other people who were with you earlier," said the manager, ". . . they assured us that you were picking up the bill for everyone." Well, we were all in one company, but not all in one department or budget, so it was a mean trick.

The next evening would have to be better, so the team went instead to an Irish pub–style restaurant. Drinks arrived, of course. After fifty minutes, however, there was no sign of food. The waitress was summoned. The food was imminent, she reassured us.

In Business in Vancouver

Another twenty minutes passed and the team asked to speak to the manager. He relayed that he was busy. A couple of other tables obviously had similar trouble because they were getting up and leaving. The team insisted that the manager present himself, which he eventually did. He explained that the waitress was new and obviously could not cope. The accused was no older than sixteen and we were outraged that the manager should blame his problems on such a young employee.

Still, as the exchange heated up, food began to appear— there was hope. But we watched the next event in horror. As an order of spareribs was being rushed into place on the table in front of my associate, when the plate stopped, the ribs kept moving, in slow motion, off the plate—gravy and all—into the lap of my colleague.

The waitress had to be commended. Realising the team was a pack of hungry lions, she quickly scooped the ribs out of his lap, back onto the plate and daintily placed it on the table. The manager—at last—realised that the meal was not progressing well and, sharp as a tack, he offered a 10-percent discount on the next visit.

His generosity was declined.

Night three, we knew, would be an improvement. Our choice was the New Yorker Restaurant, appropriately on Fifth Avenue. The dishes certainly looked appetising as we peered by candlelight at the large bifold menus. My boss, with the usual twinkle in his eye, muttered at me.

"Bill, you have a problem developing."

Now, polite teasing was always part of the team behaviour, and I replied in kind.

"You folk always give me a hard time. I've had a difficult, trying day explaining software, so now just let me enjoy dinner without any more harassment."

"You really do have a problem," insisted the lady of our team, whose husband happened to be a fire marshal. "Your menu is on fire!"

They Called Me Otherwise

Indeed my menu was in flames on the reverse side, having been held too close to the candle. It was doused with drinking water (thankfully no wine had to be sacrificed), and dinner proceeded with no further incidents.

In Business in Vancouver

Following the statistic called the "law of averages" (sic), the next night just had to be a recovery. Remember that I do not believe the laws of averages work that way; I am a statistician who works with cold probabilities and dependent or independent events.

We went to the best restaurant in town, where I spotted duck on the menu. Regrettably, it came with the dreaded "garlic smashed potatoes," then so much in vogue. I do not do garlic, so asked for a baked potato instead. The server wasn't sure and hastened off to ask the chef. No, they could not do baked potato. Well, fried potatoes? No. Rice? No. Piece of plain bread?

"You can have garlic toast if you want, sir. It's a dollar-fifty extra."

"No, no!" I protested. "I don't do garlic at all." The server went back to the kitchen and asked if they could do the duck with ungarlicked potatoes, or rice or bread, or noodles. No, this was not possible.

So I said they should just forget the carbohydrate and prepare duck with green vegetables—as long as they did not add garlic. They could not do that. The duck had to be served with garlic smashed spuds. I ate only a green salad (no dressing) and felt virtuous for avoiding that fatty other meal. (I later found out that some restaurants purchase prepackaged meals and simply microwave them. That could have been the case here. So the staff couldn't separate the potatoes from the duck.)

At last it was time to return home. At the departure check-in with my boss, Air Canada had the usual question.

"Travelling together? Now what do we have in adjacent seats?"

My supervisor shot back, "He's bad news, I don't want to travel with him. Everywhere he wanders, things go wrong." The shocked attendant, not knowing the team ribbing which had occurred all week, put me and boss in different rows.

"Flight on time?" I queried.

"We haven't heard otherwise," was the oblique reply. Although this was technically true, apparently they did know that the flight had not yet left Vancouver, an hour away. It could not possibly be ready for boarding in 40 minutes, unless the 737s had unhooked their noses, spread their wings and were fitted with Olympus 593 engines with afterburners.

When the airline finally announced that there would be a couple of hours delay, my supervisor marched up to the wicket and said, "See, I told you it was a disaster whenever I travel with him."...

That boss retired, and eventually it also became necessary to retire the software we had grown between 1984 and 2000. Fortunately, I was to be on the project to set up the new system, Oracle by name. But I was in the U.K. at the project start and missed out on setting up a budget.

I returned to find that I was in charge of the technical side of it, and that the allotted budget was totally inadequate for all the changes required. Imagine an automobile chassis and an engine. If one decides to replace the engine with a different kind and shape, then none of the other bits—steering, transmission, fuel supply, cooling—would line up correctly with the new one.

That was my problem. I had all these heritage (old) computer systems to handle payroll and sales, but their outputs looked nothing like that required for our new general-ledger engine.

I explained to the team and my bosses that the job could not be done, because we did not have enough computer programmers to change all the peripheral pieces. Not surprisingly, this did not go over well, since the budget was fixed and approved. I was told to find a way to "think outside the box." I could whine and whinge all I wanted, my choices were to admit defeat before I started, or to somehow just do it. The Scot in me remembered passing the Eleven-plus exam when I was meant to fail, running a race as an unpromising, but not quite so hopeless, athlete.

In Business in Vancouver

I was fortunate to have some talented team members and we decided to try something completely different. The technical term is "middleware," but that's unimportant. The concept is that we would leave all the peripheral pieces, for example the payroll and the sales programs, as they were. We would build one middleware program which changed all the other interfaces to what we needed. The much more experienced professional consultants were sceptical and downright worried. Sometimes I would see them in huddled conference and they would stop talking when I entered the room.

The technical team was rapidly becoming the pariah squad. To make matters worse, one night while away in Prince George, my gall bladder decided it wanted to retire and I ended up in hospital. This was just what I needed—project interruption and more stress.

If the consultants were concerned, I remained sure that my solution was the only possible one to get the whole project up and running in the short allotted time span. My middleware answer carried a big risk, but the alternative, I knew, was certain failure. My colleagues supported me and eventually our group bootstrapped itself from pariah status to heroes, as we unequivocally met our performance target. We had luck, we had tenacity, we triumphed. Our robust solution is still in place years later and performs flawlessly hundreds of times every day.

If I retire today, I will be sure that the career-aptitude test I took at the end of my Witwatersrand years had failed to tap into my talent for software solutions. My satisfaction at accomplishing what other people told me I couldn't is its own revenge—and reward.

CHAPTER NINE

Family Foibles in Vancouver

Melanie's Cakes With a Difference

These stories occupy the same time span (post–1978) as the previous set of more business-related incidents, but focus on the silly times we enjoyed as a family. In Vancouver, we were to benefit from a much closer relationship with family than would have occurred had I taken up a string of postdoctoral appointments hither and yon after graduating from Queen's University. . . .

Already a great cook, Melanie became famed for her cakes. She has baked an upright grandfather clock, hockey fields, the EXPO 86 site and, for brother Stewart the radio ham, a cake shaped and looking like a ham, though not a ham stew. People travel light years from galaxies previously unknown to place special orders for her cakes. Everything is edible. Take for example the swimming pool cake. The "water" was jelly with blue food colouring and 7-Up. The diving board was a wafer biscuit. Little birthday girls and boys are always charmed by the themes of her creations.

Melanie's grandfather-clock cake

Family Foibles in Vancouver

Melanie's fame and talents made it therefore natural for her to bake and decorate the cake to celebrate her parents' 50th wedding anniversary. A second tier was reserved for another occasion, the visit of Uncle Innes, my mother-in-law's brother.

Stewart was serving this cake when the group became aware of some excitement and tittering.

"I'm not sure there will be one for everyone. Are there enough to go around?"

Noses and eyes were levelled at the cake to observe small worms wriggling to and fro. Now in many families, the word "Gross!" would be shouted as people fled the table in horror, or even terror.

Not here. Innes the physicist, Father the zoologist, Elly the food sciences expert, David the geneticist and Melanie the biologist all wanted a closer look at said worms. It could only happen in a scientist's family.

Daughter Fiona inherited the family genes to make her interested in all things biological. She captured a grub from the cake and kept it in a jar for a few days, watching as it morphed from larva to fly. In the ensuing days, the family teased Melanie for not having kept the edge sealed to protect the cake. Father called in an entomologist who, after setting a graduate student to investigate, was able to pronounce that Fiona's new captive pet was a *diptera musca domestica*, the complex name for a common house fly.

Our memory of the worms faded and before long we were again eating Melanie's cookies with relish. Well, perhaps not actually with relish, but at least with enjoyment. Never let it be said that her baking was not excellent, worms or no worms.

Around Christmastime, my office often had cakes put out around the coffee machine. I had a fine baker in the house, so I asked Melanie for an office contribution, which was gladly granted. The fruit squares with icing on the top, sprinkled with almond slivers, were popular and I mentioned this in gratitude when I came home that December 22nd.

"I baked them a while back and had them in the freezer, so it was no bother," said Melanie. "In fact, I took my cake which you so disparagingly mocked, scraped off the worm area at the edge and froze the rest. I figured that even if any were still around, they'd catch their death of cold. When you asked for office biscuits, I just resurrected the cake mix, cooked it up thoroughly, and added icing and almonds."

That story never made it to the office.

The worm turns in the postscript to this story. Melanie's punning ham cake, mentioned above, was made for Stewart the ham-radio enthusiast on the occasion of aging 50 years to perfection. His cake was found to have four-inch-long gelatin-candy worms in it. They were much more disgusting to the scientists than the real grubs from the prior cake.

Fermions les Bosons ("Let Us Now Close Down the Bozos")

Now, you would think that one occasion of embarrassing myself in front of a physicist would be enough, but this time I exacted my own revenge. Son Alex showed an interest in the sciences and subscribed to the magazine *Discover*. There was a challenging article on subatomic particles called "Fermions and Bosons" which I read one afternoon. A couple of days later I found myself at the parent-teacher evening for my younger daughter, Natasha, at her French immersion school.

The school is in a well educated community and the parents collectively held a dense mass of degrees. After the meeting, a bearded man was gauging interest in a demonstration of his physics "tricks" to the *sixième niveau* pupils. He was a professor of physics, but he was also busy because he had important meetings in Switzerland on a regular basis. Nevertheless

Family Foibles in Vancouver

perhaps, if the school wanted, he could find time in his busy schedule to demonstrate some optical phenomena, such as light rays being bent by prisms and lenses. This couldn't be the next week, because he was away in Switzerland, and it couldn't be three weeks away because he would be in Switzerland then too, but if the school would suggest a day between these trips, perhaps he could fit it in.

The schoolteacher demurred a while, probing the level at which such demonstrations would be given.

"Well, of course I wouldn't be too technical for a junior-school science class," responded the well-barbered professor.

I had been waiting a while to talk with the teacher and butted in. "Perhaps in that case you would be better to leave out detailed exploration of fermions and bosons behaviour when addressing the grade-six class?"

The physicist was startled. "How do you know about fermions and bosons?" Then he recovered. "Ah, a fellow physicist, obviously. Have we met before? I don't believe we have."

I was reminded in a flash of my grandfather's explanation that his old-school badge was from a juvenile delinquent institution. As a Scot, I could not resist this opportunity to push over the pedestals and make us equals, so I smiled thinly and replied, "I'm an accountant."

The Weeks That Were

With my scientific empiricist training, I don't believe in coincidences. Events just happen with whatever probability and frequency they do. I certainly don't believe in adages like, "Things often happen in threes."

Cousin Maria called a few days after Natasha had been playing with her daughter. There had been head lice in the school and her daughter had been exposed. After examining

Natasha's gorgeous long red tresses, Maria was able to pronounce the verdict "lousy." Daughter Fiona turned out to be lousy too. That was event one.

Fiona was at that time perfecting her driving skills and took the opportunity for further practice. She went off to purchase more of the special shampoo. On returning home, she brushed too close to a wooden step in the driveway. The valve on the tyre caught and was ripped out completely. The air whooshed out, allowing me to practise my tyre-changing skills while the girls dealt with lice. Event two.

The day progressed. Melanie went to the freezer, intending to put the pillows in it, an effective way to freeze lice and lessen their spread. Upon opening the lid, she was greeted by various items floating in pools and puddles. Ice cream and water moved in slow backwaters, gently sloshing around the freezer compartment. A circuit breaker had tripped and there had been no power to the freezer for several days. Event three.

On an earlier and equally memorable occasion, son Alex decided during a morning shopping expedition that he could fly, and launched himself out of a shopping cart. Alas, his wings were not yet powerful enough and he fell to the supermarket's concrete floor with a crack. Event one.

Later, eating some peas for lunch, he managed to insert one into his tiny nostril. The emergency ward hospital doctor said he would probably eventually sneeze it out, which is what happened. That was event number two.

The same week, we decided to visit the Vancouver Aquarium, where they thoughtfully had provided a small pool of water with sea creatures that children could touch. There was a starfish and a few clams. Alex, who had not inherited his share of family biologist genes, was persuaded to tentatively touch the starfish, poor tortured creature. A neighbouring clam, sensing invasion, clamped on the minuscule finger close by and would not let go. Event three. Three simple cases of probability, I maintain.

Mr. Galloway's Garden and Mrs. Rabbit

Most families have some of those unexplainable weeks and most, wisely, choose to forget them. Our family decided to repair wounds and shattered prides by enjoying dinner out. We arrived home (there should be an English word "arrove") to find the neighbour's rabbits enjoying their own dinner in our family vegetable plot. This was too much.

The neighbour had his own vegetable garden, and it had chain-link fence around it, buried deep into the ground, so as to prevent such animals eating his crops (perhaps he also had electrified cables and attack wolves). There was much running around the garden, whooping and cajoling at the unfortunate rabbits, until it was almost completely dark, and the spectacle all the more comic. One rabbit was caught and put in a large sack.

Later, the second bunny was running just in front of me. I knew it and so did the rabbit. Wee Alex was just a foot in front of the rabbit, but it did not see him. With danger behind, it used the full power of its hind legs to jump. It launched straight into Alex's back. It bowled him over and finished his day. The rabbit was stunned and lay still.

Having apprehended both the neighbour's pets, we deposited them over the chain link fence, inside their owners' vegetable garden, where they could not have failed to make up for their excitement by devouring his carrots and cabbages.

The neighbour probably did get his vegetables back eventually—in the form of rabbit stew.

The Floating Keys

Children do grow up and eventually we were able to leave ours to fend for themselves in Vancouver, while we travelled. A life-insurance policy that paid out in 1992 financed a holiday. We hired a narrow boat on the Leeds–Liverpool Canal in the U.K., meeting up with our good wine friends, loyal since the days at Saint Andrews. But before joining Matthew and Sue with a crate of wine and culinary boating provisions, we had the small detail of returning the rental car.

It had been rented from a well known agency, and was to be returned to Leeds on a Saturday afternoon. Thinking that the office just might be closed, I had phoned to verify hours, and was assured that the office was open all day Saturday. After all, would I not expect that from an international car-hire firm? I would and I did, and I was suitably reassured.

Around 12:45 p.m., we arrived at the agency, which happened to be at the railway station. There was absolutely nowhere to park within a mile of the station, and to make matters worse, the office was closed. It was not just siesta time; this office was closed until the following Monday.

At about that time, someone was seen entering the office, so Melanie went to worry this person. Alas, the office really was closed and had been for forty-five minutes. The agent had just returned to collect a forgotten item.

"Office is open all day on Saturday," I argued through the car window while irate motorists behind me honked.

"Office is closed at noon on Saturday," retorted the agent.

I yelled back, insisting that I had checked and been reassured that the office was open.

"Office is closed; just leave the car in one of our parking spaces and we'll deal with the paperwork on Monday," offered the agent. I glanced across at all those nonexistent parking spaces and decided to leap into action.

The keys were in the door to the office. I snatched the keys and then asked the agent to help spy out a parking slot. She was reluctant. I waved her keys and indicated I would exchange them for helping return the car. She could only accede.

It was not what she had planned for her Saturday afternoon.

My act was quite out of character, but effective nevertheless. It is possible that by delaying her, I positioned her in the correct space-time coordinates for her to be the fortunate person to win the big lottery; or perhaps an admirer was about to pop the question of marriage and would have missed her, had she not been thus held up. And then she would not have had such lovely children and enjoyed such a happy life subsequently. One never knows.

Once aboard the narrow boat, we were given strict instructions on how to use the specified key to open the swing bridges across the canal. A fee was payable should we drop the key into the canal, so being university educated and experimentally inclined, we thought to tie a wine cork onto the key. We tested it in the kitchen sink. Sink the key still did, so we added a second wine cork. Finally, we required the corks from two regular bottles plus a bottle of champagne. With all three corks lashed to the key, the experimenters finally determined that the key would not sink.

Bilinguility

Back in Canada, our children were fast approaching the end of their schooling. Daughter Fiona showed great aptitude in French and so became an exchange student to Québec. To experience reciprocal hospitality, Véro came to Vancouver and I was keen to demonstrate my bilinguility (yes, I know the word is "bilingualism," but for me "bilinguility" has a certain panache). Lunches were being prepared, with peanut butter sandwiches a possibility. Peanut butter? *Beurre* is French for butter, and the French for peanuts begins with *ar* . . . something. I scanned the available words, and the one that popped into my mind was *araignée*. I promptly offered "spider butter" sandwiches to my guest. They were declined, but the terminology stuck in our family.

Fiona became good enough to attend Cégep (junior college) in Québec, studying all her courses in French and so she joined the Galloway diaspora. Back home, she related the story of a young lady, schooled in English, but who decided to study in French. Her comprehension was improving, but she still lapsed into translation mode instead of direct speech. Upon meeting her professor and his spouse at a shopping mall, she decided to ask in French about the progress of his academic career. "Are you doing your mistress?" she asked, and he quickly explained the difference between a master's degree and a mistress.

Night-times and Other Times in Hospitals

Granted good health for all my life so far, I do enjoy my food, and chocolate profiteroles with lashings of cream is my favourite dessert. One Christmas lunch a few of us from work had a splendid feast, including unlimited desserts. A day later I ended up in hospital with gallstone problems. The gall bladder had to be removed, so I was admitted for surgery.

I had given up coffee years ago and am also a long-distance runner, so my heart rate is normally relatively low. Given no stimulants such as caffeine, my resting beat of below 46 per minute is quite usual. I had been given narcotic painkillers following surgery, so was drowsy, comfortable, but not unconscious when a night nurse came to check on me.

She felt for a pulse, felt again and then went to hurry from the ward. I asked if the hospital was busy.

The nurse turned sharply and suddenly asked, "You're awake! You seem quite rational."

I concurred, and asked why I should not be.

The nurse by this time realised that indeed I was not in a severely hallucinogenic frame. She muttered something about my heartbeat being so low that she should call in a code on me under normal circumstances. It seems it was between 40 and 42 beats.

Family Foibles in Vancouver

"No, I'm not dead yet," I laughed. It was like the scene from the Monty Python skit, "Bring Out Your Dead."

Having a low heart rate may be an advantage. Sister-in-law has an adage that everyone is allocated a number of heartbeats to last a lifetime. A heart with a slow beat, like a long-stroke engine, pumps slowly, so the machine should last a long time.

At an earlier time in our lives, Alex was a small boy and in hospital for surgery. The anxious parents wondered if they could stay by his bed in case he wanted them during the night. The nursing staff assured us that he would be fine and that they would call at any time, if he wanted his parents. So, with the boy asleep, the family went home.

About two in the morning, the phone rang. There was a gargling sound, with some faltering breathing. Mom reassured, "Just hang on, darling, I'll be right there as quick as I can!" She dressed and drove to the hospital, where she gained immediate admission to the ward.

The night staff, however, assured her that the boy had been asleep all the time. In fact, since he was hooked up to various tubes, it would not have been possible for him to get out of bed and call home.

So Mom returned home puzzled, until she realised that we had been victims of a crank, obscene caller. Wonder what that person thought of the "Hang on, darling!" message?

Where Were You That Day?

In 2001 Wullie and Melanie flew to South Africa for a holiday celebrating his sister Catherine's birthday. It was a time to renew the African connection in a couple of ways. The family really is spread now, among North America, Scotland and South Africa, and it becomes more difficult to maintain all the links.

They Called Me Otherwise

One of the several celebrations was a visit to a game park—a very African experience—where they viewed a magnificent grown elephant from just fifteen metres. Accommodation was particularly comfortable and the meals excellent at Manyane Lodge in Pilanesberg, one of the largest national parks. One dinner combo plate was crocodile, kudu (a sort of buck) and ostrich. They enjoyed all of this, together with a very fine South African Pinotage red wine. At their chalet in the morning they breakfasted on pawpaw (papaya to North Americans) while the camp ostrich, fully two metres tall, stalked nearby, and monkeys could be seen and heard, chattering in nearby trees.

Wullie was reminded of much earlier visits to the vast African game parks, including one as a child with his family. At the lion park, he spotted a sign by the dusty road that read: "If lions eat car tyres, visitors are advised to drive on slowly." Here he had learned to spell "tyre." The British colonial influence was and still is strong in Africa.

On a much later visit, with his own child Natasha, they had elected to go on a night safari. A game warden drove them in an open-sided truck, and fortunately they had been warned to bring blankets because the African veld can be chilly. A couple of hours into this venture, word came via the two-way radio that lion had been spotted close by. The ranger drove quickly and expertly to that area. Wullie, Natasha and the other tourists could hear them. Suddenly the headlights picked out gleaming eyes, and simultaneously a roaring cacophony erupted from all around. They had come between a mother lioness and her cubs, and she was letting the intruders know that this was very rude.

The safari party was instructed to bang the sides of the vehicle; as they did so the ranger screamed the engine, in an attempt to make the lioness back off. But hell hath no fury like a lioness separated from her cubs. The ranger deftly reversed the truck into the total darkness behind,

Family Foibles in Vancouver

and the roaring abated. This was Africa, unforgettable for Natasha.

Over the years, each of the children had had the African experience and Wullie remembered them all, including his two elder children, Fiona and Alex, playing with lion cubs. The 2001 trip had been for Melanie, and too soon it was time to return to Canada.

The journey home for Wullie and Melanie from Johannesburg to Vancouver was routed via London. They decided to stop over in the U.K. long enough to celebrate their own thirtieth wedding anniversary on September 9. After landing in London, they connected up to Manchester to join fellow Scottish winebibbers Matthew and Sue from Saint Andrews University days. The U.K. couple arranged a marvellous celebration with several former university and school friends, and a party took place for a couple of days in Bridge North, near Manchester. Then Wullie and Melanie were driven to Manchester Airport, to board a connecting flight to London Heathrow.

Two events marked that day. The first occurred in Terminal 4 at Heathrow, where a man approached Wullie and asked if he were a Galloway. It was true, Wullie had to admit.

"Ah!" said the stranger. He knew Wullie's son, a bagpiper, and had seen Wullie around back in Canada, with his apparently renowned Alex.

Now that's fame! Wullie's not well known, even in his own context, but mention his bagpiper son and suddenly Wullie became internationally famous. Over eight million in London, and Wullie meets the one who knows his son from Canada....

As to the second event, do you recall what were you doing on 9/11/2001?

Wullie and Melanie were in Heathrow Airport, awaiting their flight home to Vancouver, when they heard a strange announcement in the airport departure area:

"The meeting at the World Trade Center has been cancelled."

This was, Wullie thought later, a huge understatement. They were told to collect their baggage, go away and call the airline some other time, since all flights to anywhere had been grounded. Many hours elapsed before Wullie and Melanie could retrieve their luggage.

The next issue was where to find food and accommodation. It was almost impossible to access a phone in the airport chaos, but finally they did. Sue and Matthew, having seen the news coverage, had been expecting a plea for help, and they directed Wullie to call other good friends of theirs who lived near London Gatwick Airport, in Surrey, who were willing to assist. Wullie had about four hundred pounds total in a Bank of Scotland account on the Haymarket—near where he had met Melanie thirty-one years earlier. It was enough for only one-and-a-half nights' accommodation near the airport, so he was particularly grateful for the contact.

The flight to Vancouver on that September eleventh had been scheduled to leave Heathrow at 4 o'clock, but it was close to 8 o'clock before Wullie could finally dial the Gatwick-area number he had been given. Alerted to the predicament, the friends were awaiting his call, and Wullie was heartened to hear a welcoming voice answer the phone with:

"Surrey Refugee Centre. May I help you?"

On Friendship

When we set off by bus from Heathrow Airport on the night of September 11, we still had little idea of what had actually happened in New York, Washington and Shanksville. Only during that bus ride, several hours after the World Trade Center attacks, did we begin to understand the magnitude of the situation. In fact, we spent another 11 days in the U.K. before we were able to obtain seats home.

Family Foibles in Vancouver

What luck! We used some of our pounds sterling to go to London one day, and while we thought lunch would be too extravagant, a pot of tea and a cake each at Fortnum & Mason's was a lovely post–wedding anniversary celebration, plus a happy acknowledgment of our own safety. Our hosts in Surrey made us very welcome, echoed by news stories from Gander, Newfoundland of Canadian families making stranded Americans welcome, and friendships springing up among the twin-tower ashes. Our good wine friends Matthew and Sue came down to make up a household of three couples enjoying a mid-September Indian summer.

Eventually flights were available and, almost two weeks late, Wullie and Melanie returned to Vancouver. On the landing approach, with a very clear evening sky, the twin mountains called The Lions that guard Vancouver Harbour welcomed them home, reminding them that they had travelled far. . . .

A couple of years later, these same friends journeyed with us to France, where we hired a boat for a week on the Canal du Midi. We found some perfectly drinkable wine for two and a half Euros a bottle, and some even more drinkable and slightly more expensive bottles too.

The French summer was exceedingly hot at 46 degrees Celsius, so the crew on *La Garrigue,* Canal du Midi, was forced to drink more wine than usual in order to keep cool.

Despite this thirst, we journeyed back to England with about 100 bottles of wine in the car boot, headlights pointing to the stars. It all passed duty-free, since Britain and France are both Common Market countries. We took about ten bottles back home to Vancouver, but since some were priced at only four Canadian dollars, the total duty payable was minimal. Chant de Cigales has been a favourite wine ever since. . . .

I end these anecdotes of my travels in life with that account of a fun trip. That's what life is really about: meeting with good friends and family, sharing a glass and a story. The family tales come after the business ones, and that forces one

They Called Me Otherwise

to ask the questions about retirement. I don't think I will ever retire, I'll just change priorities. I may not work for pay, but I can't live life without new challenges, without new roles in the theatrical production of life.

More than ever, I do not accept the pigeonholes in which others have tried to place me. Against expectations, I found I can pass mathematics exams and program computers. I can run, be a diplomat or a chief executive. If some have failed to acknowledge my worth, or recognise me at all, that's their problem, not mine.

As we so-called "baby boomers" move into our senior years, we'll find many more and apparently convenient labels offered to us: no longer agile; not so quick-witted; with diminished buying power; requiring more health services. I resist those labels. I'll act my own roles, not those that others expect or want me to play; I'll aspire to be what I want.

What are those aspirations? I will run further, maybe ten miles instead of five. The hopeless athlete still has no style, but this Wullie has determination to be as fit as possible, heading into the time of life called third age. There are other mountains to climb, like learning French thoroughly, because my granddaughters speak it fluently. One was heard to whisper: "Grampa speaks French with a very funny accent."

And since we own a beautiful full-size grand, I'd like to learn to play the piano. . . . Life is only just beginning.